LIBRARY SKILLS ACTIVITIES FOR THE PRIMARY GRADES

Ready-to-Use Projects and Activities for Grades 1–4

Ruth V. Snoddon

THE CENTER FOR APPLIED RESEARCH IN EDUCATION
West Nyack, New York 10995

*To my husband, Murray, for his personal
support, help, and encouragement.*

Library of Congress Cataloging-in-Publication Data

Snoddon, Ruth V.
  Library skills activities for the primary grades.

  1. School children—Library orientation. 2. Elementary school libraries—Activity programs. I. Title.
Z675.S3S658 1987   025.5'678222   87-13235

ISBN 0-87628-106-4

THE CENTER FOR APPLIED
RESEARCH IN EDUCATION
BUSINESS & PROFESSIONAL DIVISION
A division of Simon & Schuster
West Nyack, New York 10995

Printed in the United States of America

ABOUT THE AUTHOR

Ruth V. Snoddon, M.A., Northern Michigan University (Marquette), B.A., Laurentian University (Sudbury, Ontario), has been involved in elementary education for over twenty-five years as a library resource teacher and a classroom teacher in grades one through eight. She was responsible for setting up and organizing one of the first library centers built in Sault Ste. Marie, Ontario; compiled a policy manual for school library resource centers; and served as chairperson of the library committee for several years.

Mrs. Snoddon has also worked on a number of curriculum development committees, is co-author with Nancy M. Hall of *Guided Research Discovery Units* (The Center, 1983), and author of *Ready-to-Use Library Skills Games: Reproducible Activities for Building Location and Literature Skills* (The Center, 1987).

In 1987, Mrs. Snoddon was granted an award for *Library Skills Activities for the Primary Grades: Ready-to-Use Projects and Activities for Grades 1–4,* by the Federation of Women Teachers' Associations of Ontario. The Federation selected this book as being a very useful resource for teacher librarians.

ABOUT THIS BOOK

Library Skills Activities for the Primary Grades is designed for teachers and librarians to use with students in grades 1–4. These completely organized projects and related activity pages give students practice in basic library use and further development of research skills.

For easy use in selecting the projects and related activities, the book has been organized into the following three main sections:

Section I	LEARNING ABOUT OUR LIBRARY
Section II	ANIMALS AROUND THE WORLD
Section III	LANDS AND PEOPLE OF THE WORLD

Each section contains five research reports, project instructions, and activity pages that are relevant to the topics. All pages can be duplicated as many times as needed for use by individuals, small groups, or the entire class.

Section I provides primary children with the opportunity to use simple reports to find out more about their library, work with alphabetical order, and practice note-taking skills. Sections II and III give students more opportunities to expand and develop their knowledge of the library by working with a variety of resource materials such as atlases, dictionaries, encyclopedias, and nonfiction books while researching an animal, the lands, or the peoples of the world.

The activity pages that accompany each section can be used along with the research reports to expand on the topic, or they can be used separately. This provides more flexibility and variety throughout the book so that you can adapt to the needs of the individual student.

You will find that *Library Skills Activities for the Primary Grades* can be used effectively to:

- Assist in developing language, geography, research, and reading skills through the use of interesting topics and activities
- Create a resource activity center
- Develop or supplement a unit of study
- Motivate students to read books and explore topics that may be, but are not necessarily, curriculum-related
- Provide meaningful and challenging activities in an interesting way for the entire classroom, small groups, or individuals

A special feature of this book is the Activities/Skills Index that lists all the projects and activity pages as well as the appropriate grade level and the skill involved.

The projects and activity pages presented in *Library Skills Activities for the Primary Grades* will provide a continuing source of ready-to-use materials that will enhance, enrich, and reinforce your classroom and library program.

Ruth V. Snoddon

ACTIVITIES/SKILLS INDEX

Activity Pages to Accompany
Section I ● 53

SECTION II
ANIMALS AROUND THE WORLD • 77

To the Teacher • 78

Activity Pages to Accompany
Section II • 133

Activity Pages		Grade Level	Skill Involved
II-1	Animals of Africa	3-4	Alphabetization
II-2	Animals of Asia	3-4	Alphabetization
II-3	Animals of Australia	3-4	Alphabetization
II-4	Animals of North America	3-4	Alphabetization
II-5	Animals of South America	3-4	Alphabetization
II-6	Pets Around the World	1-3	Alphabetization
II-7	Animal Storybook Report	3-4	Book reporting
II-8	Any Pet in the World	2-4	General language
II-9	African Animal Bookmark	2-4	Book reporting
II-10	Asian Animal Bookmark	2-4	Book reporting
II-11	Australian Animal Bookmark	2-4	Book reporting
II-12	North American Animal Bookmark	2-4	Book reporting
II-13	South American Animal Bookmark	2-4	Book reporting
II-14	Pet Bookmark	1-4	Book reporting
II-15	Animals and the Continents They Live On	3-4	Encyclopedia usage
II-16	Mammals of Africa	3-4	Crossword puzzle
II-17	Mammals of Asia	3-4	Crossword puzzle
II-18	Mammals of Australia	3-4	Crossword puzzle
II-19	Mammals of North America	3-4	Crossword puzzle
II-20	Mammals of South America	3-4	Crossword puzzle
II-21	Pets Around the World	2-4	Crossword puzzle
II-22	Favorite Animal Poem	2-4	Book reporting
II-23	My Favorite Wild Animal	1-4	Book reporting
II-24	Elephant	2-4	General language
II-25	Planning a Diorama	3-4	Book reporting
II-26	Making a Diorama	3-4	Book reporting
II-27	Mix-Up Mania: Animals of Africa	2-4	Puzzle
II-28	Mix-Up Mania: Animals of Asia	2-4	Puzzle
II-29	Mix-Up Mania: Animals of Australia	2-4	Puzzle
II-30	Mix-Up Mania: Animals of North America	2-4	Puzzle
II-31	Mix-Up Mania: Animals of South America	2-4	Puzzle
II-32	Mix-Up Mania: Pets Around the World	1-4	Puzzle
II-33	Regions Where Animals Live	3-4	Research
II-34	Find the African Mammals	3-4	Word Search
II-35	Find the Asian Mammals	3-4	Word Search
II-36	Find the Australian Mammals	3-4	Word Search
II-37	Find the North American Mammals	3-4	Word Search
II-38	Find the South American Mammals	3-4	Word Search
II-39	Find the Pets	1-4	Word Search

SECTION III
LANDS AND PEOPLE OF THE WORLD • 173

To the Teacher • 174

Projects	Grade Level	Skill Involved
Research Report #15: Famous People Around the World	2-4	Book reporting
15-1 Project Instructions		
15-2 The Person I'm Writing About		
15-3 About the Person		
15-4 At Home or Abroad?		
15-5 Family Life		
15-6 The Person's Accomplishments		
15-7 Other Interesting Facts		
15-8 Bibliography Page		

Activity Pages to Accompany
Section III • 223

Activity Pages	Grade Level	Skill Involved
III-1	Books About People	3-4	Book reporting
III-2	Clothing People Wear	2-4	Research
III-3	A Map of the Library	1-3	Map reading
III-4	Library Floor Plan	3-4	Map reading
III-5	A Map of Agricultural Products	3-4	Map reading
III-6	A Map of Natural Resources	3-4	Map reading
III-7	A Map of Rainfall	3-4	Map reading
III-8	A Map of Your Street	1-3	Map reading
III-9	Geography Facts	3-4	Recognizing reference sources
III-10	Geography Terms	3-4	Atlas usage
III-11	Holidays Around the World	3-4	Research
III-12	Canadian Abbreviations	3-4	Atlas usage
III-13	Eastern U.S. Abbreviations	3-4	Atlas usage
III-14	Western U.S. Abbreviations	3-4	Atlas usage
III-15	National Landmarks	2-4	Research
III-16	Plan a Menu	3-4	Research
III-17	Africa Puzzle Pleasers	3-4	Puzzle
III-18	Asia Puzzle Pleasers	3-4	Puzzle
III-19	Australia Puzzle Pleasers	3-4	Puzzle
III-20	Europe Puzzle Pleasers	3-4	Puzzle
III-21	North America Puzzle Pleasers	3-4	Puzzle
III-22	South America Puzzle Pleasers	3-4	Puzzle
III-23	Quick Quiz on Africa	3-4	Research
III-24	Quick Quiz on Asia	3-4	Research
III-25	Quick Quiz on Australia	3-4	Research
III-26	Quick Quiz on Europe	3-4	Research
III-27	Quick Quiz on North America	3-4	Research

LEARNING ABOUT OUR LIBRARY

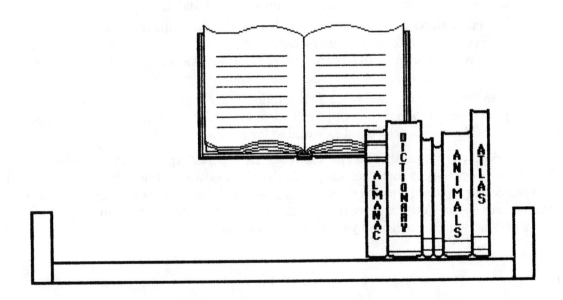

TO THE TEACHER

This section contains several simple reports for the beginning researcher as well as practice in developing note-taking skills and writing in proper bibliographic form. The reports become progressively more difficult so that the skills developed will be useful for the more experienced students as they go on to the research reports presented in Sections II and III.

Each report is self-explanatory, although teacher and librarian assistance may sometimes be necessary. Depending on the knowledge already possessed by your students, you may use the reports for review, or to assist your students in acquiring new skills. Individual pages within some reports can also be used alone if a student does not need to do a complete report, or you can substitute from the activity pages that follow the reports.

Here are the five research reports in Section I:

- Research Report #1, "Learning About Our Library," gives primary children the opportunity to familiarize themselves with their library in a simple way. It is suitable for grades 1–3.

- Research Report #2, "Fun With Our ABC's," gives primary students practice in arranging in alphabetical order as it relates to the library center. It is suitable for grades 1 and 2.

- Research Report #3, "Learning More About Our Library," continues where Research Report #1 left off. Students must first identify the types of materials in their library, and then are introduced to fiction and nonfiction books and the card catalog. This report is suitable for grades 3 and 4.

- Research Report #4, "Note-Taking Knacks," gives tips on how to choose a topic, organize information using cards, and prepare a simple bibliography. It also provides practice in writing collected information in good sentence structure. This report is suitable for grades 3 and 4.

- Research Report #5, "What Is a Bibliography?" gives students practice in preparing a bibliography in proper form for books, encyclopedias, and magazines. This research report is suitable for grades 3 and 4.

The activity pages that follow the research reports expand on the knowledge presented previously so that students gradually increase and develop their knowledge of a particular topic as it relates to the library. You will find that interchanging within the reports and activity pages will provide you with flexibility that can benefit the students' individual needs and your teaching presentation.

NAME _____   GRADE _____

Research Report #1

LEARNING ABOUT OUR LIBRARY

TEACHER _____   DATE _____

NAME _____   DATE _____

MY LIBRARY RESOURCE CENTER TEACHER

I visited my Library Resource Center today. My library resource teacher's name is:

_____ .

Draw a picture of your library resource teacher in the space below.

NAME _____   DATE _____

RULES OF MY LIBRARY RESOURCE CENTER

All libraries have rules to follow. Find out what rules you must know when you visit your library.

List the most important rules below.

1. _____

2. _____

3. _____

4. _____

5. _____

6. _____

After you have learned all the rules, take a walk around and see what kinds of things you can read and use in your library.

WHAT'S IN MY LIBRARY RESOURCE CENTER?

Visit your school library. Put a check mark next to each of the things you find there.

☐ books

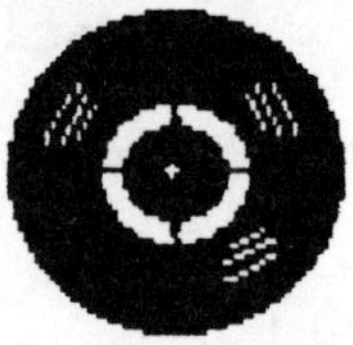

☐ filmstrips

☐ newspapers

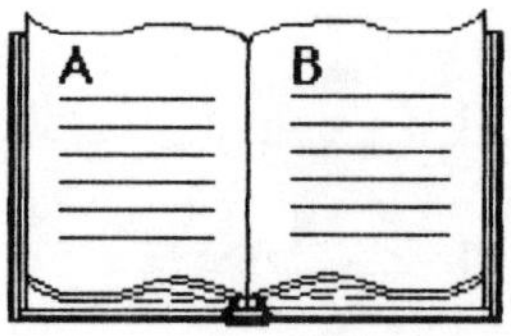

☐ magazines

☐ records

☐ pictures

☐ dictionary

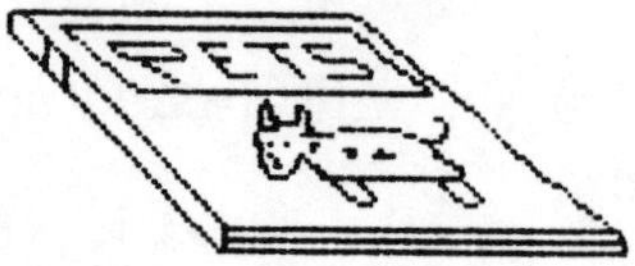

☐ computers

OTHER THINGS:

_____

_____

_____

_____

NAME _____   **DATE** _____

FICTION BOOKS

Your favorite stories or fiction books are found in one part of your library. The books are put on the shelves in alphabetical order using the authors' last names, for example:

Georgie by Robert <u>Bright</u> ← last name

Look at the books on the shelf above and find the authors' last names. Print the first letter of each name below.

_____   _____   _____   _____   _____

Now find your favorite storybook in your library resource center. Print the title of your book here:

_____

_____

Who wrote your story? Print the name of the author below. Draw a circle around the last name.

_____

NAME _____   **DATE** _____

DRAW A PICTURE

After you have finished reading your favorite story, draw a picture to show the part you liked best. Be sure to color your picture.

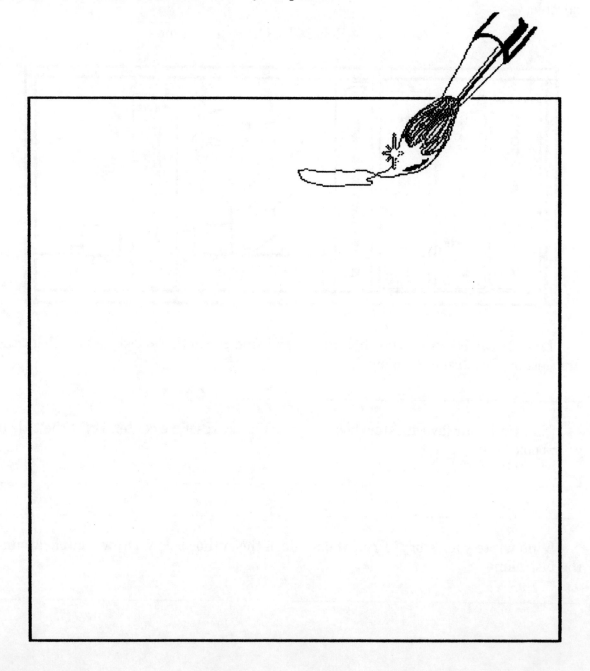

Title of Book _____

_____

Author's Name_____

NAME _____   GRADE _____

Research Report #2

FUN
WITH OUR

TEACHER _____   DATE _____

NAME _____   **DATE** _____

FIX THE ALPHABET

©1987 by The Center for Applied Research in Education, Inc.

Everything in the library is put in alphabetical order so you must know your ABC's.

Fill in the missing letter:

C __ E	R __ T	N __ P
B __ D	Q __ S	A __ C
K __ M	X __ Z	I __ K

Here are the 26 letters of the alphabet all mixed up:

A P C K H D O V I B S Z Q E N Y R L T F U M W J G X

Print them below in the proper order:

___ ___ ___ ___ ___ ___ ___ ___ ___ ___ ___ ___ ___

___ ___ ___ ___ ___ ___ ___ ___ ___ ___ ___ ___ ___

Remember the caterpillar from the top of the page? Now put its letters in the proper order on the lines below.

NAME _____   **DATE** _____

WHAT'S THE ORDER?

Let's see how well you can put these words in order. Look at the first letter of each word. Then print the words in alphabetical order.

fish   dog   cat   bird

1. _____

2. _____

3. _____

4. _____

book   title   author   teacher

1. _____

2. _____

3. _____

4. _____

desk   apple   pencil   crayon

1. _____

2. _____

3. _____

4. _____

GOOD WORK

PUT THE LETTERS IN ORDER

When we visit the library we learn that books are put in alphabetical order.

If we put these books in alphabetical order...   they will look like this.

F	H	E	G	E	F	—	—
T	S	U	R	—	—	—	—
Y	W	V	X	—	—	—	—

This is EASY. Let's go on to the next page.

NAME _____   **DATE** _____

PUT THE BOOKS IN ORDER

When we visit the library we learn that books are put in alphabetical order. See if you can put the books below in alphabetical order.

If we put these books in alphabetical order...

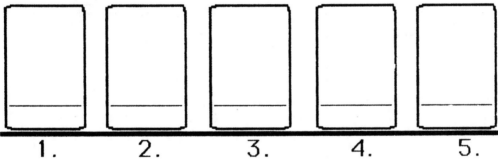

they will look like this.

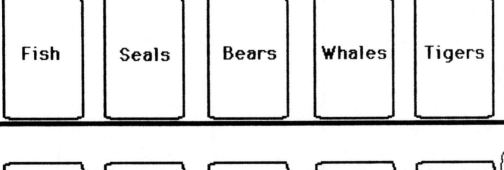

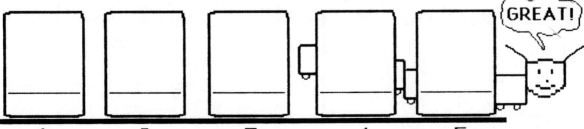

YOUR OWN THREE BOOKS

Some books in our library and classroom use alphabetical order from beginning to end. See if you can find some. Get your teacher or librarian to help you.

Draw a picture of your book below. Then print the name of the book beside it.

1.

2.

3.

©1987 by The Center for Applied Research in Education, Inc.

NAME _____   DATE _____

WHERE WOULD YOU FIND IT?

On our visits to the library we have learned that books are put in alphabetical order.

The set of books below is made up of encyclopedias. There are 20 books in the set. They are put in alphabetical order as a set. Things beginning with "A" are in the "A" book. Things beginning with "C" are in the "C" book. Some books have two or more letters. And every book has a number.

A	B	C	D	E	F	G	H	I	J–K
1	2	3	4	5	6	7	8	9	10

L	M	N	O	P	Q–R	S	T	U–V	WXYZ
11	12	13	14	15	16	17	18	19	20

Which book would you look in to find the following things? Print the number in the box:

Frogs .... ☐   Pets .... ☐   Bats .... ☐

Snakes .... ☐   Trees .... ☐   Dogs .... ☐

Cats .... ☐   Zebras .... ☐   Flowers .... ☐

I knew you could do it!

NAME _____   DATE _____

PICTURES FROM THE ENCYCLOPEDIA

Ask the teacher or librarian to show you where the encyclopedias are found in your library. They will show you the sets that you can use.

Choose one book from the set and look at it. Draw some pictures below of some of the things you looked at.

Color each drawing and print the name under each picture.

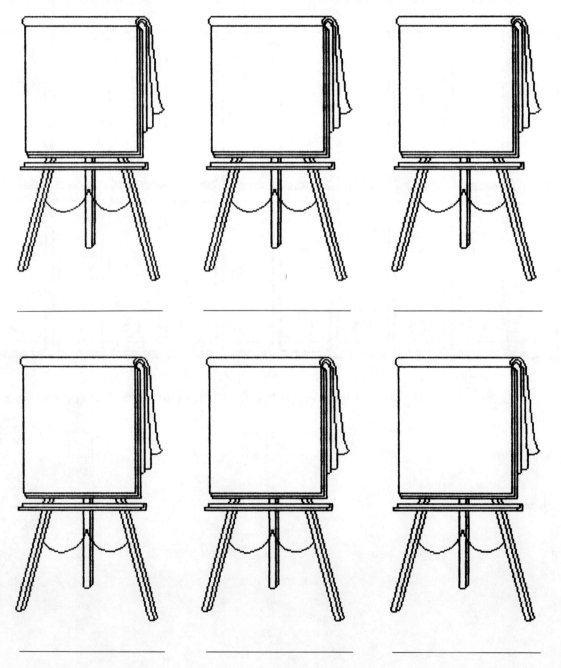

Name of Set _____   Letter _____

NAME _____ GRADE _____

Research Report #3

LEARNING MORE ABOUT OUR LIBRARY

TEACHER _____ DATE _____

NAME _____   DATE _____

A REVIEW OF THE LIBRARY

My library resource teacher's name is:

_____

Check your library to see what materials and books are there. Put a check mark by each item you find:

___ almanac   ___ globe

___ biography books   ___ magazines

___ computers   ___ maps

___ dictionaries   ___ newspapers

___ encyclopedias   ___ pictures

___ filmstrips   ___ records

List other items you found in the library:

_____

_____

_____

_____

What do you like best about your library?

_____

_____

_____

_____

NAME _____   DATE _____

ALL ABOUT FICTION BOOKS

Every library is organized so there is a place for all books and materials. Fiction books are arranged on the shelves in alphabetical order by the authors' last names. These fiction books are all mixed up on the shelf. Can you put them in order?

Lindgren	Steig	Cleary	Blume	MacGregor	Dahl
Pippi Goes to the South Seas	Amos and Boris	R I B S Y	Tales of a Fourth Grade Nothing	Miss Pickerell goes to Mars	Fantastic Mr. Fox
___	___	___	1 ___	___	___

On the lines below, write the last names of the authors in alphabetical order. Then number each book to show where it should be arranged on the shelf. The first one is done for you.

1. <u>Blume</u>

2. _____

3. _____

4. _____

5. _____

6. _____

NAME _____   DATE _____

ALL ABOUT NONFICTION BOOKS

Nonfiction books are books that contain facts about real things. They are divided into sections by the subjects that the books are about. Each section has its own set of numbers. This is part of a plan called the Dewey Decimal System.

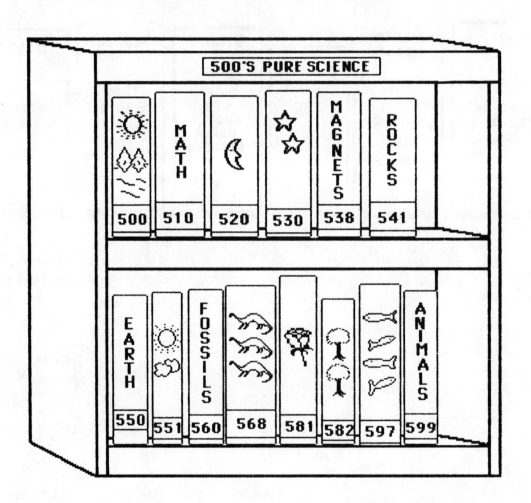

Go to the science section of your library. Choose three books. Write the title, author, and number of each book below:

Title   Author   Number

_____   _____   _____

_____   _____   _____

_____   _____   _____

You will find more than one book on each subject.

NAME _____   DATE _____

ALL ABOUT THE CARD CATALOG

Every library has a set of drawers called a card catalog. Each drawer holds many cards.

The cards give the name and author of each book in the library. Other cards give the subject of every book. Each drawer has letters on it that are arranged in alphabetical order.

Look at the card catalog below. Write the letters of the drawer you would open if you wanted books on each of these subjects. The first one is done for you.

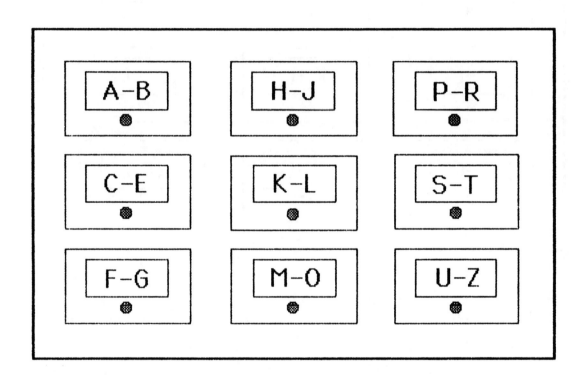

DINOSAURS	C–E	SNOW	_____
LIONS	_____	FISH	_____
PETS	_____	WHALES	_____
BEARS	_____	MAMMALS	_____

NAME _____   DATE _____

IN WHICH DRAWER?

Look at the card catalog below. In which drawer of the card catalog would you look for each author? Remember, the last name of author comes first.

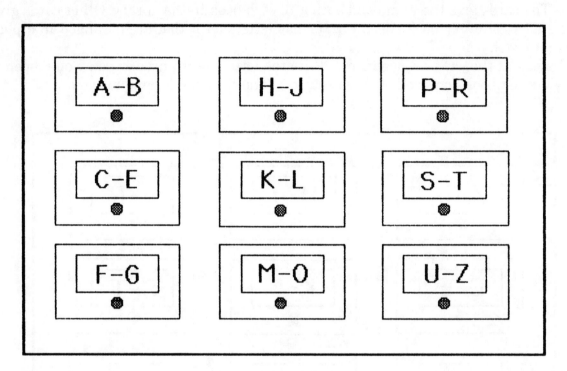

Underline the author's last name to help you, then check which drawer has the first letter of the author's last name. Write it down. The first one is done for you.

Judy <u>Blume</u>	A-B	Syd Hoff	_____
Peggy Parish	_____	Gene Zion	_____
Dr. Seuss	_____	Jane Moncure	_____
Roald Dahl	_____	Bill Peet	_____

In which drawer would you look for each title?

Wobble, the Witch Cat   _____

Tale of Peter Rabbit   _____

Harry the Dirty Dog   _____

Am I a Bunny?   _____

A SUPER DOOPER JOB!

NAME _____   DATE _____

MY SCHOOL'S CARD CATALOG

    The card catalog in your library may not look like card catalogs in other libraries. This is because libraries do not have the same books.

    Visit your school library and find the card catalog. Then draw a picture of your school card catalog in the space below. Make sure to count the drawers and draw the same number. Then write the same letters on each drawer that you see on your library card catalog.

NAME _____   GRADE _____

Research Report #4

NOTE-TAKING KNACKS

TEACHER _____   DATE _____

NAME _____   DATE _____

FINDING RESOURCES IN THE LIBRARY

In order to find information in your library you need to know how to find information in nonfiction books, encyclopedias, and other sources.

You also need to know how to organize and keep the information you have found so that you can use it for some research reports.

Use a variety of sources, such as nonfiction books, dictionaries, encyclopedias, magazines, and any other source that will be helpful as you gather information for your research reports. Look for these sources in your library.

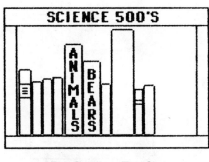

Nonfiction Books

Dictionaries

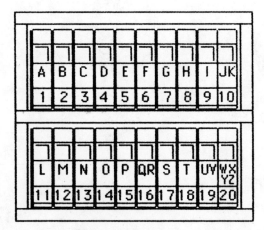

Encyclopedias

Magazines

NAME _____   DATE _____

WHAT ARE THE IMPORTANT FACTS?

As you read, look for the most useful or important facts. The detective below has put a circle around the topics and underlined the most useful or important facts to show you how it is done.

(Tigers) live from 15-20 years.

The (numbat) eats termites.

(Bats) have wings that flap.

The (blue whale's) main food is krill.

The (dingo) is a wild dog.

The (platypus) is an egg-laying mammal.

(Foxes) have large ears and long bushy tails.

An (African elephant) has the largest ears.

Now you list five of the topics with their important facts:

TOPICS   IMPORTANT FACTS

_____   _____

_____   _____

_____   _____

_____   _____

_____   _____

NAME _____   DATE _____

CHOOSING A TOPIC

When you are doing your own research report you must first choose a topic. Some boys and girls have trouble with this.

Pretend you are going to do a research report on bears. So you must then decide what kind of bear. There will be lots of choices. We call this narrowing down a topic. We only want to write on one kind of bear this time.

Which one would you write on? _____

NAME _____   **DATE** _____

MY TOPIC AND SUBTOPICS

After you have chosen your topic and narrowed it down to one kind of animal, use your research materials to gather information about it.

You can jot down facts about your animal in your own words on note pad or paper. But if you want to be really organized, use the ideas on the following pages to help you. If you want, you can use your own small cards instead.

Pretend you are going to find some facts about polar bears. That is your topic. Next, what kinds of facts do you want to find out about polar bears? These become your subtopics.

You will have one subtopic on each card. Number each card.

NAME _____   **DATE** _____

FILLING OUT SUBTOPIC CARDS

Under each subtopic jot down three or four facts about it. Remember to use your own words.

Include the name of your source as well. Give the page numbers and the author's name when you can.

Your teacher and librarian will help you if you need assistance. Sometimes they have a special way in which they would like you to list your sources. You would use this later when you do your bibliography page.

```
┌──────────────────────────────────────────────────┐
│                                   Number  1        │
│   Topic: ____Polar Bears____                       │
│   Subtopic: _____Food_____                       │
│   FACTS:                                           │
│   1. ____main food is ringed seals____             │
│   2. _____                  │
│   3. _____                  │
│   4. _____                  │
│   SOURCE: __Encyclopedia_____                   │
│   Title: _____                  │
│   Author: _____                  │
│   Page Number (s):_____                  │
└──────────────────────────────────────────────────┘
```

Complete this card for practice.

©1987 by The Center for Applied Research in Education, Inc.

NAME _____   DATE _____

TAKING MORE NOTES

Sometimes you have to use more than one source for a subtopic in order to get three or four facts about it. Then you must use more than one card. Make sure you number each card so you will know how many you have used.

Practice by doing another card on polar bears. This time use a different source to find out about the subtopic, food.

Number __2__

Topic: __Polar Bears__

Subtopic: ____Food____

FACTS:
1. _____
2. _____
3. _____
4. _____

SOURCE: _____
Title: _____
Author: _____
Page Number(s):_____

Complete this card for practice.

NAME _____   **DATE** _____

NOTE-TAKING KNACKS

Practice your note-taking skills by using the information from your cards on polar bears to write a brief note about the food of the polar bear. This time use the facts, and write in proper sentences.

THE POLAR BEAR

_____
_____
_____
_____
_____
_____
_____
_____
_____
_____
_____
_____
_____
_____

Your teacher or librarian will help you if you need assistance.

Supplementary Pages

for

Research Report #4

NAME _____   DATE _____

ELEPHANT TALK

Practice your note-taking skills by using the topic, elephants. Read about elephants in an encyclopedia or nonfiction book and write four facts about each kind. The first card has been started for you.

```
┌────────────────────────────────────────────────────┐
│                                   Number  1          │
│  Topic: __Elephants_____                        │
│  Subtopic: __African_____          │
│  FACTS:                                              │
│  1. _____             │
│  2. _____             │
│  3. _____             │
│  4. _____             │
│  SOURCE: __Encyclopedia_____             │
│  Title: _____            │
│  Author: _____            │
│  Page Number(s):_____            │
└────────────────────────────────────────────────────┘
```

```
┌────────────────────────────────────────────────────┐
│                                   Number  2          │
│  Topic: _____                │
│  Subtopic: _____        │
│  FACTS:                                              │
│  1. _____             │
│  2. _____             │
│  3. _____             │
│  4. _____             │
│  SOURCE: _____            │
│  Title: _____            │
│  Author: _____            │
│  Page Number(s):_____            │
└────────────────────────────────────────────────────┘
```

NAME _____   DATE _____

ELEPHANT FACTS

Practice your note-taking skills by using the information from your cards on the two kinds of elephants. Write a note using the facts that you have gathered on each. Be sure to write it in your own sentences.

ELEPHANTS

_____

_____

_____

_____

_____

_____

_____

_____

_____

_____

_____

_____

_____

_____

Your teacher or librarian will help you if you need assistance.

NAME _____   DATE _____

TIGER, TIGER

Practice your note-taking skills by using the topic, tigers. Choose one kind of tiger to find information on. Think of four subtopics to gather facts on. The first two cards have been started for you.

Number __1__

Topic: _____

Subtopic: __FOOD_____

FACTS:

1. _____

2. _____

3. _____

4. _____

SOURCE: __Encyclopedia_____

Title: _____

Author: _____

Page Number (s): _____

Number __2__

Topic: _____

Subtopic: _____SIZE_____

FACTS:

1. _____

2. _____

3. _____

4. _____

SOURCE: _____

Title: _____

Author: _____

Page Number (s): _____

NAME _____ DATE _____

TIGER, TIGER
(continued)

Try to use different sources. Your teacher or librarian will help you if you need assistance.

Number __3__

Topic: _____

Subtopic: _____

FACTS:

1. _____
2. _____
3. _____
4. _____

SOURCE: _____

Title: _____

Author: _____

Page Number(s): _____

Number __4__

Topic: _____

Subtopic: _____

FACTS:

1. _____
2. _____
3. _____
4. _____

SOURCE: _____

Title: _____

Author: _____

Page Number(s): _____

NAME _____ DATE _____

TIGER FACTS

Practice your note-taking skills by using the information from your cards on the tiger. Write a note using the facts that you have gathered on it. Be sure to write it in your own sentences.

_____ TIGER

NAME _____   DATE _____

EXTRA CARDS FOR NOTE-TAKING KNACKS

These cards may be cut out and numbered in order. Ask your teacher to duplicate several pages of these for you when you are doing a research report.

Number ____

Topic: _____

Subtopic: _____

FACTS:

1. _____
2. _____
3. _____
4. _____

SOURCE: _____

Title: _____

Author: _____

Page Number(s): _____

Number ____

Topic: _____

Subtopic: _____

FACTS:

1. _____
2. _____
3. _____
4. _____

SOURCE: _____

Title: _____

Author: _____

Page Number(s): _____

EXTRA NOTE PAGE FOR NOTE-TAKING KNACKS

NAME _____   GRADE _____

Research Report #5

WHAT
IS A
BIBLIOGRAPHY?

BIBLIOGRAPHY

ENCYCLOPEDIAS

1. "Africa." World Book Encyclopedia, 1

    Vol. 1, 88.

2.

Write it down

TEACHER _____   DATE _____

NAME _____   **DATE** _____

INFORMATION SHEET

A bibliography is a special way of listing all the sources you have used while researching a topic in the library.

To make a bibliography easier, begin it while you are finding the information on your topic. Your teacher or librarian will help you get started by showing you the form and punctuation you should use.

The following pages in this report will give you practice in preparing a bibliography for sources such as books, encyclopedias, and magazines.

BIBLIOGRAPHY

BOOK

1. Black, Susan. <u>Bears, Bears, Bears</u>. New York: Broadway Press, 1987.

ENCYCLOPEDIA

1. "Polar Bears." <u>Animal Lover Encyclopedia</u>, 1986, Vol. 12, p. 216-217.

MAGAZINE

1. Travers, Ruth. "The Incredible Polar Bear." <u>Animal World</u>, May 1987, p. 5-8.

NAME _____   DATE _____

BOOKS AS A SOURCE

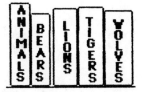

For a book, the following information is needed when writing a bibliography:

1. the author's name (last name first)
2. title of book (underlined)
3. city of publication
4. name of publisher
5. last copyright date
6. pages you found useful if you did not read the entire book

Author   Title   City

BOOKS
1. Black, Susan. <u>Bears, Bears, Bears.</u> New York: Broadway Press, 1987, p. 24-26.

Publisher   Copyright Date   Pages

Pretend that you are doing a research report. Pick your own topic. Find one book you could use and list it below as part of your bibliography.

BIBLIOGRAPHY

BOOKS

1. _____

_____

_____

What topic did you choose? _____

NAME _____   DATE _____

ENCYCLOPEDIAS AS A SOURCE

A	B	C	D	E	F
1	2	3	4	5	6

For an encyclopedia, use the following information when writing a bibliography:

1. title or subject of the article (in quotations)
2. encyclopedia name (underlined)
3. last copyright date
4. volume number
5. pages used for reference

Title of Article   Encyclopedia Name

ENCYCLOPEDIAS

1. "Polar Bears." Animal Lover Encyclopedia, 1986, Vol. 12, p. 216–217.

Copyright Date   Volume Number   Pages

Pretend that you are researching a topic. Pick out one encyclopedia that will give you information on it. List it below as part of your bibliography.

BIBLIOGRAPHY
ENCYCLOPEDIAS

1. _____

_____

_____

What topic did you choose? _____

DID YOU REMEMBER EVERYTHING?

NAME _____   DATE _____

MAGAZINES AS A SOURCE

For a magazine, use the following information when writing a bibliography:

1. author (if known), last name first
2. name of article (in quotations)
3. name of magazine (underlined)
4. date when magazine was published
5. pages used for reference

                    Author   Name of Article

MAGAZINES

1. Travers, Ruth. "The Incredible Polar Bear." Animal World, May 1987,
   p. 5-8.

Pages   Name of Magazine   Date Published

Pretend that you are researching a topic. Pick out one magazine that will give you information on it. List it below as part of your bibliography.

BIBLIOGRAPHY
MAGAZINES

1. _____

   _____

   _____

What topic did you choose? _____

DON'T FORGET TO CHECK YOUR PUNCTUATION.

NAME _____   DATE _____

NEWSPAPERS AS A SOURCE

For a newspaper, use the following form when writing a bibliography:

1. title of article (in quotations)
2. name of newspaper (underlined)
3. date of publication
4. section
5. page number

Title of Article   Name of Newspaper

NEWSPAPER

1. "Amazing Polar Bears." Daily Star, 15 June 1987, sec. 2, p. 7.

Date of Publication   Section   Page

Pretend that you are researching a topic. Pick out one newspaper that will give you information on it. List it below as part of your bibliography.

BIBLIOGRAPHY
NEWSPAPER

1. _____

_____

_____

What topic did you choose? _____

©1987 by The Center for Applied Research in Education, Inc.

NAME _____   DATE _____

OTHER SOURCES

For sources such as films, filmstrips, records, and tapes, use the following form when writing a bibliography:

1. title of source used (underlined)
2. producer of source used
3. copyright date

Title   Producer

FILMSTRIP

1. Polar Bears. Animal Lover Films, Inc., 1986.

Copyright Date

Pretend that you are researching a topic. Pick out two sources, other than books, that will help you. List them below as your bibliography.

BIBLIOGRAPHY

_____

1. _____

_____

_____

_____

2. _____

_____

_____

What topic did you choose? _____

Supplementary Pages

for

Research Report #5

NAME _____   DATE _____

ALL ABOUT ELEPHANTS

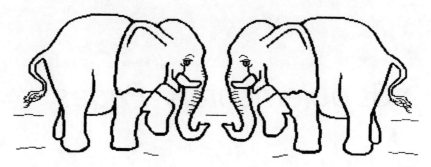

Practice writing a bibliography page using the proper form. Read about elephants in two nonfiction books. List your sources below in alphabetical order.

BIBLIOGRAPHY—ELEPHANTS   No. _____

BOOKS

1. _____

  _____

  _____

  _____

  _____

2. _____

  _____

  _____

  _____

  _____

Your teacher or librarian will help you if you need assistance.

NAME _____   DATE _____

ALL ABOUT TIGERS

Practice writing a bibliography page using the proper form. Choose one kind of tiger to find information on. Use one encyclopedia, and one nonfiction book as your sources. Write up the bibliography page below.

BIBLIOGRAPHY—TIGER   No. _____

BOOK

1. _____

_____

_____

ENCYCLOPEDIA

1. _____

_____

_____

Your teacher or librarian will help you if you need assistance.

EXTRA BIBLIOGRAPHY CARDS

These cards may be cut out and numbered in order. Use a separate card for each kind of source. Your teacher will duplicate as many as you need.

BIBLIOGRAPHY   No. _____

_____

1. _____

_____

_____

2. _____

_____

_____

BIBLIOGRAPHY   No. _____

_____

1. _____

_____

_____

2. _____

_____

_____

Activity Pages

to

Accompany Section I

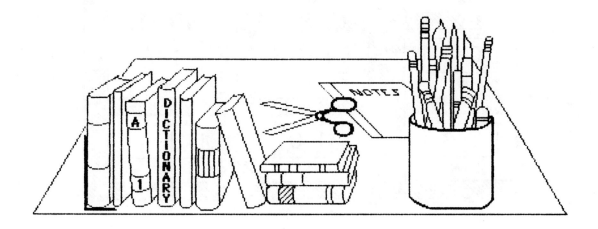

NAME _____   DATE _____

FIND THE MISSING LETTERS

Every library has a set of drawers that holds many cards. We call this a card catalog.

Find the card catalog in your library. Have your librarian show you some of the cards. Look at the letters of the alphabet on the front of each drawer.

Now look at the card catalog below. Check each drawer. Some drawers don't show every letter of the alphabet on the front. Can you fill in the missing letters?

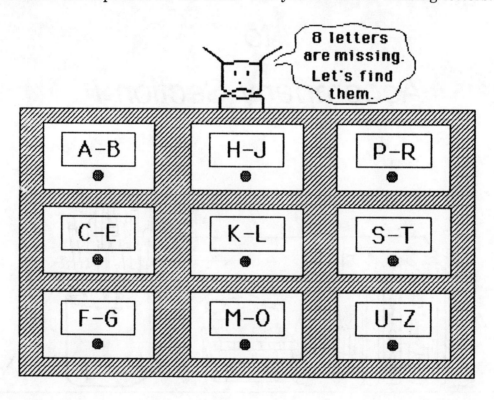

The first one is done for you.

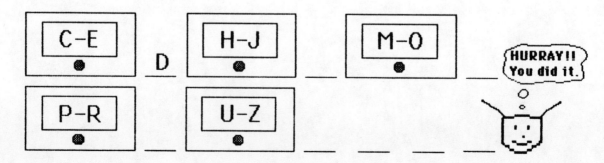

NAME _____   DATE _____

FIND THE DRAWER

Inside each drawer of the card catalog are many cards. They help us find the books in our library. You may look for a book by its title, by the author's last name, or by the subject of the book.

Look at the card catalog below. Then see if you can write the correct letters for the drawer you would look in for each question below.

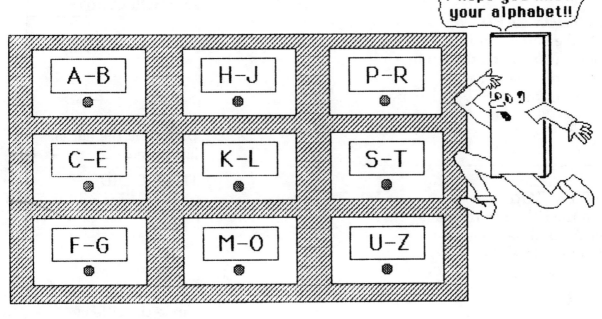

I hope you know your alphabet!!

In which drawer would you look for each title?

Tales of a Fourth Grade Nothing _____

Freddy the Detective _____

Charlotte's Web _____

Week Mom Unplugged the TVs _____

In which drawer would you look for each author?

Donald Sobol _____   Jean Little _____

Judy Blume _____   Joan Nixon _____

Judith Viorst _____   Syd Hoff _____

Did you remember to look at the author's LAST name??

In which drawer would you look for each subject?

COMPUTERS _____   TIGERS _____

PENGUINS _____   BASEBALL _____

GEOGRAPHY _____   JOKES _____

NAME _____   DATE _____

THREE KINDS OF CARDS

What does 398.2 GAL stand for?

Be sure to find out.

The card catalog has three kinds of cards to help you find books in the library. They are the author card, title card, and subject card.

Cut along the dotted line below. Cut out each card and paste it in the proper box so it correctly matches the definition.

AUTHOR CARD
On the author card the author's name is found on the top line of the card. The last name is written first.

AUTHOR CARD

Underline the author's last name.

TITLE CARD
On the title card the name of the book is found on the top line. The title is also listed below.

TITLE CARD

Circle the title of your book.

SUBJECT CARD
The subject card gives the subject heading for the book first. It will be found on the top line in capital letters.

SUBJECT CARD

What is the subject of the book? _____

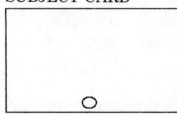

FAIRY TALES
398.2   Galdone, Paul.
GAL   Cinderella.

398.2   Galdone, Paul.
GAL   Cinderella.

           Cinderella.
398.2   Galdone, Paul.
GAL   Cinderella.

NAME _____   DATE _____

CHOOSING THE BEST SOURCE

There are many kinds of reference books to choose from in the library. Draw a line from the picture to the correct definition of each source below.

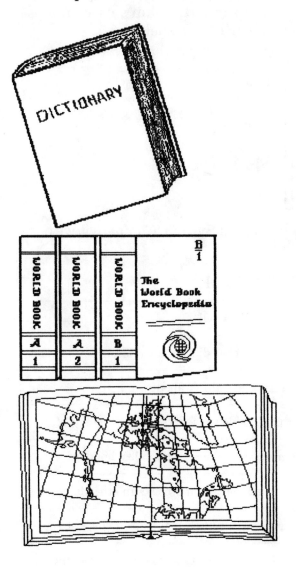

A book that gives us true facts about persons, places, things, events, and ideas is called an _____ .

An atlas is a book that contains a collection of maps.

A book that gives us an alphabetical listing of words and their meanings is called a _____ .

ATLAS, DICTIONARY, or ENCYCLOPEDIA

Which reference source would you choose to answer the following questions?

What is the meaning of "difficult"? _____

What is the capital of Maine? _____

When was John Kennedy born? _____

What is the population of Canada? _____

NAME _____   DATE _____

THE DEWEY DECIMAL SYSTEM

Nonfiction books in your library all have numbers and letters marked on each book spine. These numbers and letters are taken from a plan made up by a man named Melvil Dewey. He divided all nonfiction books into ten main subject groups so that all books on the same subject would be together on the shelf.

Check your library for a chart of the Dewey Decimal System. Compare it with the one below.

DEWEY DECIMAL SYSTEM

NUMBER	GROUP NAME	WHAT BOOKS ARE ABOUT
000-099	GENERAL WORKS	Many subjects (Encyclopedias, other reference books, etc.)
100-199	PHILOSOPHY	Books on things people think about
200-299	RELIGION	Books about God, Bible stories, Greek mythology, etc.
300-399	SOCIAL SCIENCES	Books on community helpers, fairy tales, holidays, etc.
400-499	LANGUAGES	Books such as dictionaries, and books in other languages
500-599	PURE SCIENCE	Books on astronomy, weather, plants, animals, fish, etc.
600-699	APPLIED SCIENCES	Books on energy, transportation, space, pets, cooking, etc.
700-799	FINE ARTS	Books on art, drawing, hobbies, games, magic, sports, etc.
800-899	LITERATURE	Books on poetry, plays, etc.
900-999	HISTORY	Books on countries, famous people, flags, history, etc.

Find all ten groups in your library. On the line below, write the title, author, and call number for a book from the Fine Arts section.

_____

NAME _____ DATE _____

FINDING SOME FINE ARTS BOOKS

Melvil Dewey gave all his nonfiction books a number from one of the ten groups so that the books could be arranged on the shelves in proper order. We call this method the Dewey Decimal System of Classification. He also divided the ten main groups into different subject areas, each with a set of numbers.

FINE ARTS 700 - 799

Here are sets of numbers for some subjects in the 700's.

Books on ART	Books on Drawing	Books on MUSIC	Books on SPORTS
700–709	740–749	780–789	790–799

Go to the Fine Arts section of your library. Find two books each on art, drawing, music, and sports. Write the title, author, and call number of each book below:

ART BOOKS

Title	Author	Call Number
_____	_____	_____
_____	_____	_____

DRAWING BOOKS

Title	Author	Call Number
_____	_____	_____
_____	_____	_____

MUSIC BOOKS

Title	Author	Call Number
_____	_____	_____
_____	_____	_____

SPORTS BOOKS

Title	Author	Call Number
_____	_____	_____
_____	_____	_____

NAME _____   DATE _____

DRAW A BOOK COVER

Visit your library and read one of your favorite fiction books. Use the book below and draw a picture on the cover to show us what the book was about. Then print the title of your book and the author's name on it.

Print the name of the author below. Draw a circle around the last name.

_____

Can you find other books in your library by the same author? If you can, print the titles below or on the back of this sheet.

_____

_____

NAME _____   DATE _____

DO YOU KNOW ABOUT FICTION BOOKS?

Look at the fiction books below and see if you can answer the questions about them.

1.   2.   3.

  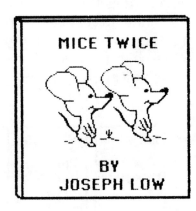

Print the title for each book.

1. _____

2. _____

3. _____

Print the author's name for each book. Then put a circle around the author's last name.

1. _____

2. _____

3. _____

On the lines below, print the last names of the authors in alphabetical order.

1. _____

2. _____

3. _____

I knew you could do it!

Your teacher or librarian will be glad to help you.

I-9

NAME _____   DATE _____

MIXED-UP FICTION BOOKS

We already know that fiction books are arranged on the shelves in alphabetical order by the author's last name. However, if there are two or more books by the same author, they are then arranged in alphabetical order by title.

These fiction books are all mixed up on the shelf. Can you put them in the correct order? Cut out the books at the bottom of the page and paste them in the proper place so they will be in alphabetical order according to title.

Don't forget! When a title starts with the same word, look at the second word.

WELL DONE!

©1987 by The Center for Applied Research in Education, Inc.

| HAYWOOD Eddie's Menagerie F HAY | HAYWOOD Betsy and Billie F HAY | HAYWOOD Away went the Balloons F HAY | HAYWOOD Eddie's valuable property F HAY | HAYWOOD Halloween Treats F HAY | HAYWOOD B is for BETSY F HAY |

| HAYWOOD Eddie's Menagerie F HAY | HAYWOOD Betsy and Billie F HAY | HAYWOOD Away went the Balloons F HAY | HAYWOOD Eddie's valuable property F HAY | HAYWOOD Halloween Treats F HAY | HAYWOOD B is for BETSY F HAY |

NAME _____   DATE _____

LOOK AT THIS INDEX

Sometimes when we visit the library we want books that give us information on many things.

When we choose a book that gives us facts we should look at the back of it to see if it has an index. An index can help us find what we want to read about without having to look at the whole book.

HOW AN INDEX WORKS
1. It lists each SUBJECT in the book and the PAGE where it is found.
2. The SUBJECTS are listed in alphabetical order.

Now look at this index from a book and see if you can answer these questions about it:

INDEX

bats, 6
bears, 14-17
beavers, 13
camels, 10
deer, 7
elephants, 20-21
giraffes, 19
lions, 18,
mammals, 1-5
monkeys, 22-23
seals, 12
skunks, 11
zebras, 24

1. On what pages would you read about mammals?

   _____

2. On what page would you read about bats?

   _____

3. On what pages could you find information about elephants?

   _____

4. Would you find information on birds in this book?

   _____

5. What would be a good title for this book?

   _____

Don't forget! An INDEX is found in the back of a book.

NAME _____   DATE _____

MORE ABOUT AN INDEX

Some books that give us facts about many subjects have an index in the back to help us. The index lists each subject in the book and the page where it is found. The subjects are listed in alphabetical order. Study the index page below and then use the index to answer the questions.

INDEX

Bears, kinds of
    black, 5
    brown, 6
    grizzly, 7
    polar, 8

Eating habits
    how bears eat, 11
    what bears eat, 11,12
    when bears eat, 12

Enemies, 3

Finding food
    by feeling, 13
    by seeing, 13
    by smelling, 14

Friends, 3

Size
    biggest bear, 4
    smallest bear, 4

I WONDER? Can I find anything on the Teddy Bear?

1. On what page will you find information on the grizzly bear? _____

2. Name two kinds of bears you will find information about in this book.

_____ and _____

3. What subject heading do you look under to find out which bear is the smallest?

_____

4. Would you find information on the Teddy Bear? _____

Write down the names of two animals you enjoy reading about. They are:

_____

Now visit your library and find some books about these animals. Check to see if the books have an index. Try and use it to help you find things to read about in each book. If your books do not have an index, look for others that may have one and use them instead.
Get your teacher or librarian to help you if you need assistance.

I'm glad I know how to use an INDEX. I can find what I want to read about in a hurry!

NAME _____   DATE _____

FINDING OUT ABOUT PETS

Books that give us only facts and information are called nonfiction books. Find a nonfiction book about pets in your library.

Print the title of your book.

_____

Print the author's name below.

_____

What is the call number for your book?

_____

After you have read your book, draw a picture of your favorite pet in this box.

Print two facts that you learned from reading your book. Use good sentences.

1. _____

2. _____

Get your teacher or librarian to show you where to find the pet books if you can't find them yourself.

NAME _____   DATE _____

PUT ON YOUR NONFICTION THINKING CAP!

Read this page carefully. It will help you understand how nonfiction books are arranged on the shelves.

> Nonfiction books are put on the shelves according to their numbers. Books with lower numbers begin on the left and the numbers get higher as you go to the right. The number is on a label found on the spine of each book.

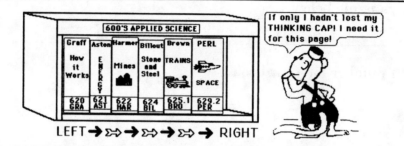

> Under the number of a nonfiction book you will find the first letters of an author's last name. It may be one or more. How many letters were used on the label of each book above? _____

Look at the shelf above and write the author's last name for each call number. Then circle the first three letters of each name.

621
AST _____

629.2
PER _____

620
GRA _____

624
BIL _____

622
HAR _____

625.1
BRO _____

> When a decimal is used in the call number, the book is still filed in order by the number. For instance, all the 636's would come before the 637's. The numbers might be 636.1, 636.2, 636.3, up to 636.9. Then the 637's would start.

Now write down the number that comes first.

629.6 or 629.2 _____   796.9 or 794 _____

398.2 or 398.8 _____   917.4 or 918 _____

Get your librarian to help you if you have a problem understanding this page.

NAME _____ DATE _____

MATCH THE BOOK PARTS

Do you know the parts of a book? Cut along the dotted line below. Cut out each book part and paste it in the box so it matches correctly.

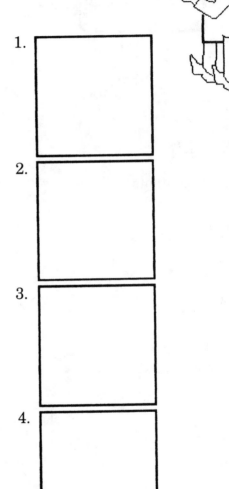

BOOK PARTS

1. The table of contents gives us a list of the chapters in a book.

2. The title page lists the author's name, the name of the book, and the illustrator.

3. The index page is an alphabetical list of the topics found in a book.

4. The spine of the book is the part you see when the book is on the shelf.

1.

2.

3.

4.

INDEX
cats 5-6
dogs 7-10
fish 11-13
hamsters 14-16
horses 17-20
rabbits 21-24
turtles 25-26

CONTENTS
Title	Page
1. Cats and Dogs	5-10
2. Fish	11-13
3. Hamsters	14-16
4. Horses	17-20

NAME _____   DATE _____

MIXED-UP BOOK PARTS

The BOOK PARTS and matching PHRASES are all mixed up. Can you draw a line from the BOOK PART to the right PHRASE so they will be correct?

BOOK PARTS

1. table of contents

2. title page

3. chapters

4. cover

5. dedication page

6. copyright page

7. index

PHRASES

groups of pages book is divided into

page that shows date book was printed

list of chapters in a book

an alphabetical list of the topics found in a book

outside part of a book

mentions people who have helped the author in some way with a book

includes author's name, the name of the book, and the illustrator's name

I knew you could do it. GOOD WORK!

NAME _____   DATE _____

THE TABLE OF CONTENTS

A table of contents is found at the front of a book. It lists the chapters in the order in which they come in the book. It also gives the titles of the chapters and the page number each chapter begins on.

Look at the table of contents below and see if you can answer the questions about it.

I know the difference between an INDEX and a TABLE of CONTENTS! DO YOU?

TABLE OF CONTENTS		
Chapter	Title	Page
1	About Bears	1
2	Bear Enemies	4
3	Bear Friends	6
4	Kinds of Bears	8
5	Where Bears Live	12
6	What Bears Eat	14
7	How Bears Find Their Food	15

1. How many chapters are there in this book? _____

2. What is the title of Chapter 4? _____

3. Which chapter would tell you about the bear's home? _____

4. On what page does Chapter 2 begin? _____

Pretend that you have written a book. What would it be about?

_____

Now see if you can make a table of contents for it.

TABLE OF CONTENTS		
Chapter	Title	Page

You deserve a BOUQUET! WELL DONE!

NAME _____   DATE _____

ALL ABOUT THE TITLE PAGE

Every book in the library has a title page. This is a very important page because it gives the title of the book and the author. If a book has pictures in it, the name of the artist is also printed on the title page.

Look at the title page below, then find three books in your library and look for the title page in each book.

ALL ABOUT ALLIGATORS
BY
JOHN B. JONES

Illustrated by Ann Davis

Animal World Press New York

← ← TITLE

← ← AUTHOR

← ← ARTIST

Now draw two title pages below. You may use a book from the library to help you with one and then make up one of your own.

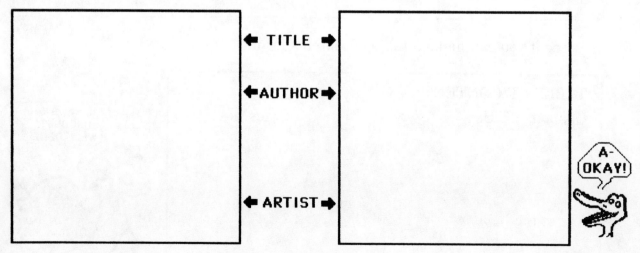

← TITLE →

←AUTHOR→

← ARTIST →

A-OKAY!

NAME _____   DATE _____

MORE ABOUT THE TITLE PAGE

Let's stop monkeying around and learn about the TITLE PAGE

A title page of a book gives the title of a book and the author's name. The name of the artist or illustrator is often given too, if the book has drawings in it.

Most title pages tell you the name of the company that issued the book. This is the publisher. You may see the name of a city also. This is the place where the publisher has its offices. Draw a line to each part below.

Title of Book

Author's Name

Illustrator's Name

Publisher

Place of Publishing

What is a MAMMAL?

by Jennifer W. Day

illustrated by ANN BREWSTER

GOLDEN PRESS   NEW YORK

Now visit your library. Choose two books and look at the title page in each. Answer these questions.

What is the title of each book?

1. _____

2. _____

What is the author's name?   Illustrator's name?

1. _____   _____

2. _____   _____

Who is the publisher?   Name the place of publishing.

1. _____   _____

2. _____   _____

GREAT WORK! I knew you could do it.

USING THE DICTIONARY

A dictionary gives us the meanings of words. It also gives us other important information that can be helpful. Look at the dictionary pages below and see what else a dictionary might give us.

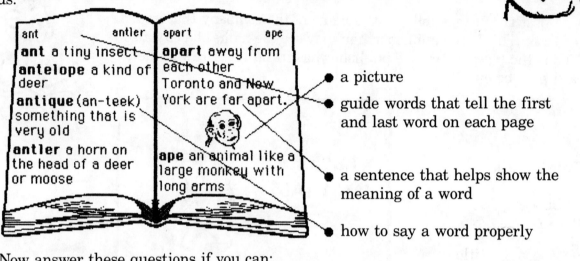

* a picture
* guide words that tell the first and last word on each page
* a sentence that helps show the meaning of a word
* how to say a word properly

Now answer these questions if you can:

1. What is the meaning of antler? _____

_____

2. What are the guide words for the left page of the dictionary? _____

_____

3. Use the word "antique" in a sentence to show the meaning. _____

_____

_____

4. Print the guide words that are found on the right page of the dictionary. _____

_____

5. Do you know what the word "pronunciation" means? _____

You may know the words "syllable" and "pronunciation" already. If not, have your teacher or librarian tell you what they mean.

A SUPER EFFORT!

NAME _____   DATE _____

USE YOUR OWN DICTIONARY

A dictionary gives us the meanings of words. It also gives us other important information that can be helpful. Read below some of the things a dictionary may provide us with:

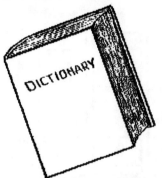

- guide words that tell the first and last word on each page
- how to say a word properly
- meaning of a word
- a picture
- a sentence that helps show the meaning of a word

Choose a dictionary from your classroom or library and see if you can answer the following questions:

1. What is the title of your dictionary?

_____

2. Who published your dictionary?

_____

3. The word you look up in a dictionary is printed in heavy, dark letters. We call this

word an _____

4. Words that start with the same letter are arranged in alphabetical order by the

_____

5. Write the words in each group in alphabetical order:
   A. cobra, coal, coat, cob, coax

   _____

   B. long, lone, log, lonely, logger

   _____

   C. six, sir, sit, sixth, site

   _____

Look at the second, third, and fourth letters of some words.

NAME _____ DATE _____

USING ENCYCLOPEDIAS

The books below are called encyclopedias. There are 20 volumes in this set. The set is arranged in alphabetical order, with each book having a letter or letters on it. These letters tell you the first letter of the subjects you will find in each volume. The subjects in each volume are also arranged alphabetically.

A	B	C	D	E	F	G	H	I	J-K
1	2	3	4	5	6	7	8	9	10

L	M	N	O	P	Q-R	S	T	U-V	WXY Z
11	12	13	14	15	16	17	18	19	20

Below is a list of subjects. On the line next to each subject print the letter or letters and the number found on the volume you would look in for that subject.

1. Giraffe _____   6. Africa _____

2. New York _____   7. Clouds _____

3. Eskimos _____   8. Machines _____

4. Yak _____   9. India _____

5. Rainbow _____   10. Peanut _____

Look up the subject "Yak" in your encyclopedia. Write what you learned about it here. _____

_____

_____

_____

Get your teacher or librarian to assist you if you need help.

©1987 by The Center for Applied Research in Education, Inc.

NAME _____   DATE _____

GUIDE WORDS IN ENCYCLOPEDIAS

Many encyclopedias use guide words at the top of the pages. These words are usually printed in dark capital letters. They are arranged in alphabetical order and can help you locate your information much faster if you know how to use them.

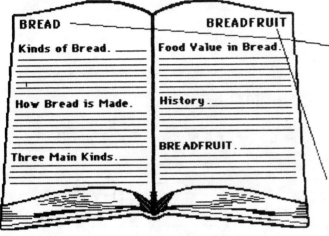

The guide word on the left page is either the subject of the first entry that appears on the page or the subject of an entry continued from the page before.

The guide word on the right page is the subject of the last entry found on the page.

Use *The World Book Encyclopedia* to answer these questions:

1. Look up the subject "Pony." What guide word is on that page?

_____ Give the page number. _____

2. Look up the subject "Sea Cow." What guide word is on that page?

_____ Give the page number. _____

What is the volume number? _____ Letters on volume? _____

Use the *Britannica Junior Encyclopedia* to answer these questions:

1. What guide word appears on the last page of the "Dog" entry?

_____ Give the page number it is on. _____

2. Look up the guide word "Weasel." What other entries are found on those pages?

_____

3. What is the guide word for the "Alpaca" entry? _____

4. What is the guide word for the "Textiles" entry? _____

Get your teacher or librarian to assist you if you need help.

NAME _____   DATE _____

FINDING FACTS IN ENCYCLOPEDIAS

PURR-FECT!

An encyclopedia gives us facts about persons, places, things, and events. Look at the subjects listed below and write down whether they name a person, place, thing, or event. The first one is done for you.

1. Ladybug _____Thing_____   6. Gorilla _____

2. Clara Barton _____   7. Cowboy _____

3. Clouds _____   8. England _____

4. Olympics _____   9. Trees _____

5. Mexico _____   10. Christmas _____

Choose three of these subjects to look up in an encyclopedia. Then fill in the information below about each.

Subject (Entry) _____

Encyclopedia Name _____

Volume Number _____ Letter or Letters on Volume _____

Year of Publication _____ Page Number Subject Found on _____

Subject (Entry) _____

Encyclopedia Name _____

Volume Number _____ Letter or Letters on Volume _____

Year of Publication _____ Page Number Subject Found on _____

Subject (Entry) _____

Encyclopedia Name _____

Volume Number _____ Letter or Letters on Volume _____

Year of Publication _____ Page Number Subject Found on _____

Does your teacher or librarian sometimes ask you to pick out a topic to look up in an encyclopedia? After doing this page you should know three other words that mean about the same as topic. Can you write them here?

Did you know that we call the SUBJECT we look up an ENTRY or ARTICLE?

ANIMALS AROUND THE WORLD

TO THE TEACHER

Section II contains the following five reports that can be used by individuals, small groups, or the entire class. Project instructions are included, along with lists of animal names that you may want to provide to students.

- Research Report #6, "Animals Around the World," guides students in researching animals of Africa, Asia, Australia, North America, and South America. Maps of Canada and the United States are also included. It is suitable for grades 3 and 4.

- Research Report #7, "Book Report Mobile," encourages students to make a simple mobile that shows the information they have learned about animals after reading a book. The report is suitable for grades 1–4.

- Research Report #8, "Animal Mobile," gives students an opportunity to present their research report as a mobile rather than as a booklet. This mobile requires students to use a variety of library sources in order to find more information than is needed for the book report mobile. It is suitable for grades 3 and 4.

- Research Report #9, "Pets Around the World," gives students a chance to write about their own experiences with pets as well as use books in the library to assist them in answering the questions. It is suitable for grades 1–3.

- Research Report #10, "Animal Diary," gives students practice in using reference sources, using their own knowledge, or using a combination of both as they pretend to be an animal for five days of their life. This is suitable for grades 3 and 4.

The activity pages that follow the research projects provide students with additional activities relevant to and associated with the animal theme. Students will need to use their dictionary and language skills, reference sources, and read a variety of books in order to complete activities on alphabetization, making bookmarks, crosswords, and word searches as well as others. Hopefully these activities will make using the library a lot of fun for the students while they learn at the same time.

NAME _____   **GRADE** _____

Research Report #6

ANIMALS AROUND THE WORLD

TEACHER _____   **DATE** _____

NAME _____   DATE _____

PROJECT INSTRUCTIONS

1. Choose an animal found on one of the continents. It may be one taken from the list provided by your teacher or librarian or you may have picked out your own.

2. Make sure when you have decided on your animal that you tell which kind it is. For example, if you choose to find information on a bear, make sure you say which kind. Do you wish to learn more about the grizzly, black, or polar bear? Follow that rule when choosing any animal if there is more than one of its kind.

3. Go to the card catalog in your library resource center and look up "Animals" or your specific animal, such as "Bears." Check your encyclopedias, science reference sets, and other nonfiction books as well for additional information.

4. Ask your teacher or librarian for assistance if you need help.

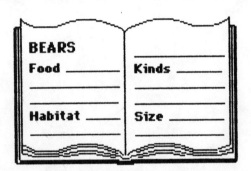 

5. Read all about the animal you have chosen. Then close your books and answer the questions. If you want, jot down bits of information on a piece of note paper first. Write or print the answers to the questions in your own sentences. Do not copy word-for-word from your reference sources.

6. Your teacher or librarian may want you to include your own title page, table of contents page, and bibliography page before handing in your report. If so, he or she will explain what you must do.

Don't forget sources such as films, filmstrips, magazines, pamphlets, and television. They may give you information about your animal, too.

NAME _____   DATE _____

ANIMALS OF AFRICA

Choose an animal from the list below or you may think of your own.

AARDVARK   HYENA
ANTELOPE   IBIS
BABOON   IMPALA
CAMEL   JACKAL
CHEETAH   LEOPARD
CHIMPANZEE   LION
CROCODILE   MAMBA
ELEPHANT   MONKEY
FENNEC   OKAPI
FLAMINGO   OSTRICH
GAZELLE   PORCUPINE
GIRAFFE   RHINOCEROS
GORILLA   SERVAL
GNU   VULTURE
HIPPOPOTAMUS   ZEBRA

NAME _____   **DATE** _____

THE ANIMAL I'M WRITING ABOUT

I chose the _____ .

It lives on the continent of _____ .

Draw an illustration of your animal.

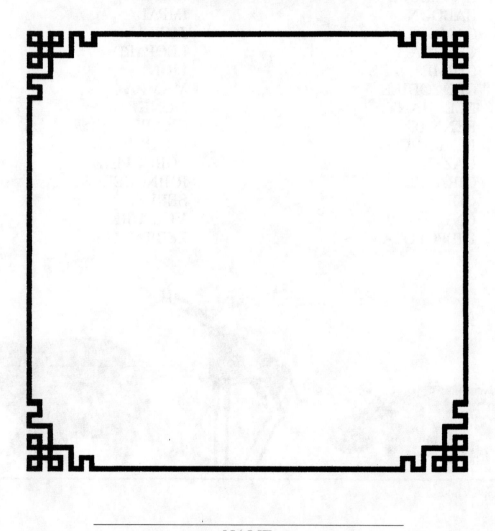

_____
NAME

NAME _____   **DATE** _____

INFORMATION ABOUT MY ANIMAL

What does your animal look like when it is full grown? _____

_____

_____

_____

_____

What is the main food of your animal? _____

_____

_____

Draw some pictures below showing what your animal
likes to eat. Print the name of each food under its picture.

NAME _____   **DATE** _____

ALL ABOUT MY ANIMAL'S HOME

Draw a picture of your animal's home.

The _____ home

Tell about your animal's home. _____
_____
_____
_____
_____
_____

Is there anything special about your animal's home? _____
_____
_____
_____

NAME _____   **DATE** _____

MY ANIMAL LIVES IN AFRICA

In what part of Africa does your animal live? _____

_____

_____

_____

_____

_____

Show on the map below where your animal lives in Africa.

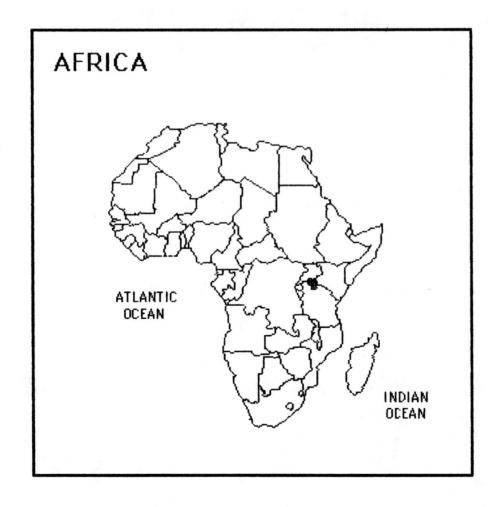

Substitute Pages

for

Research Report #6

ANIMALS OF ASIA

Choose an animal from the list below or you may think of your own.

ANOA	MONGOOSE
BACTRIAN CAMEL	MURRE
BLACK BEAR	MUSK DEER
BROWN BEAR	ONAGER
CARACAL	ORANGUTAN
CIVET	ORYX
DROMEDARY	PANDA
ELEPHANT	REINDEER
GIBBON	RHESUS MONKEY
HORNBILL	RHINOCEROS
IBEX	SIBERIAN TIGER
KARAKUL	TARSIER
KOMODO DRAGON	WATER BUFFALO
LEMMING	WATER DEER
LEOPARD	YAK

NAME _____   DATE _____

ANIMALS OF AUSTRALIA

Choose an animal from the list below or you may think of your own.

BANDICOOT   PLATYPUS
CUSCUS   RAT KANGAROO
DINGO   RED KANGAROO
DUGONG   SALT-WATER CROCODILE
ECHIDNA   SUGAR GLIDER
EMU   TASMANIAN DEVIL
FAIRY PENGUIN   TASMANIAN WOLF
KOALA   TREE KANGAROO
KOOKABURRA   WALLABY
LYREBIRD   WOMBAT

NAME _____   **DATE** _____

ANIMALS OF NORTH AMERICA

Choose an animal from the list below or you may think of your own.

ALLIGATOR	MOUNTAIN LION
BADGER	MOUSE
BALD EAGLE	MUSK OX
BEAR	OPOSSUM
BEAVER	PORCUPINE
BUFFALO	PRAIRIE DOG
CARIBOU	PRONGHORN
CHIPMUNK	RABBIT
DEER	RACCOON
FOX	SEA LION
GILA MONSTER	SEAL
GOPHER	SKUNK
LEMMING	SQUIRREL
MOOSE	WOLF

NAME _____   DATE _____

ANIMALS OF SOUTH AMERICA

Choose an animal from the list below or you may think of your own.

ALPACA	MANED WOLF
AGOUTI	MARMOSET
ARMADILLO	MARSH DEER
BLACK CAIMAN	PARROT
BUSH DOG	PECCARY
CAPYBARA	PENGUIN
CAVY	PUMA
CHINCHILLA	RHEA
COATI	SLOTH
COYPU RAT	SPECTACLED BEAR
GIANT ANTEATER	TAPIR
GUANACO	TREE PORCUPINE
IGUANA	VAMPIRE BAT
JAGUAR	VICUNA
LLAMA	YAPOK

NAME _____   **DATE** _____

PETS AROUND THE WORLD

Choose an animal from the list below or you may think of your own.

ALLIGATOR   LIZARD
BURRO   MOUSE
CAT   PARAKEET
DOG   PIG
FROG   RABBIT
GERBIL   RACCOON
GOLDFISH   ROOSTER
GUINEA PIG   SNAKE
HAMSTER   SPIDER
HORSE   TOAD
LAMB   TURTLE

NAME _____ DATE _____

MY ANIMAL LIVES IN ASIA

In what part of Asia does your animal live? _____

_____

_____

_____

_____

_____

Show on the map below where your animal lives in Asia.

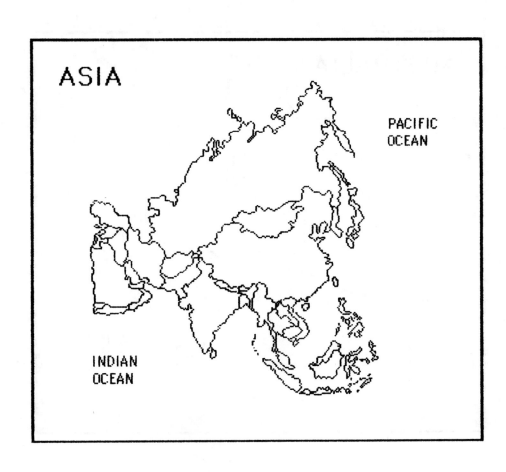

6-6S

NAME _____ DATE _____

MY ANIMAL LIVES IN AUSTRALIA

In what part of Australia does your animal live? _____

_____

_____

_____

_____

Show on the map below where your animal lives in Australia.

NAME _____   DATE _____

MY ANIMAL LIVES IN NORTH AMERICA

In what part of North America does your animal live? _____

_____

_____

_____

_____

_____

Show on the map below where your animal lives in North America.

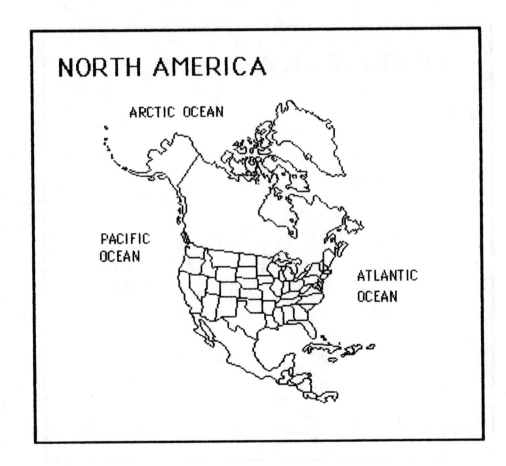

NAME _____   **DATE** _____

MY ANIMAL LIVES IN SOUTH AMERICA

In what part of South America does your animal live? _____

_____

_____

_____

_____

Show on the map below where your animal lives in South America.

NAME _____   DATE _____

MY ANIMAL LIVES IN CANADA

In what part of Canada does your animal live? _____

_____

_____

_____

_____

_____

Show on the map below where your animal lives in Canada.

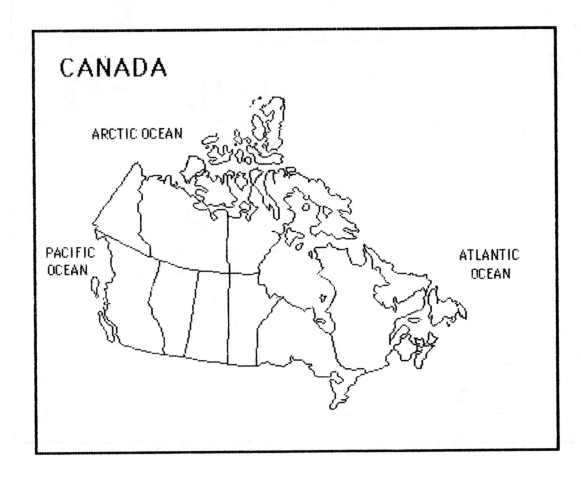

NAME _____   DATE _____

MY ANIMAL LIVES IN THE UNITED STATES

In what part of the United States does your animal live? _____

_____

_____

_____

_____

Show on the map below where your animal lives in the United States.

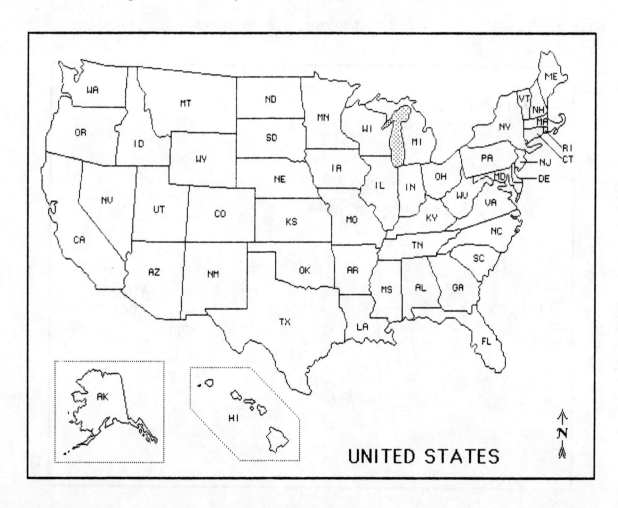

NAME _____   GRADE _____

Research Report #7

BOOK REPORT
MOBILE

TEACHER _____   DATE _____

NAME _____   **DATE** _____

DIRECTIONS FOR MAKING
A BOOK REPORT MOBILE

Choose an animal to do your research report on. This report will be made into a mobile.

1. Pick out a book that will help you answer the questions found on each mobile design.
2. Read all you can about the animal you have chosen to research.
3. Try to answer the questions as best as you can.
4. Print or write as neatly as you can in good sentences.
5. Color your designs.
6. Cut around your designs and glue them onto construction paper.
7. When the glue has dried, carefully cut out each design.
8. Punch a hole in each outline. You will need a hole at the bottom of the book design, too.
9. Tie strings or yarn through each hole.
10. Tie strings to the hanger.
11. Hang your mobile on display.

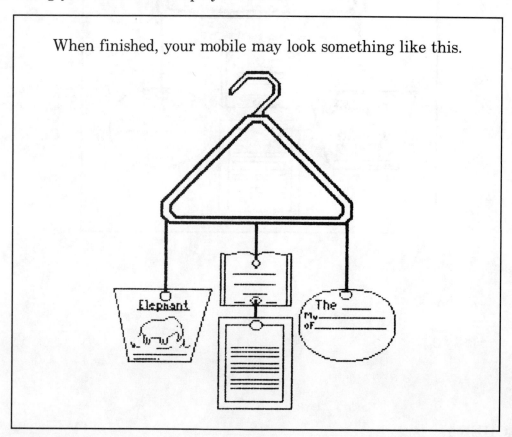

When finished, your mobile may look something like this.

NAME _____ DATE _____

BOOK REPORT MOBILE
Design #1

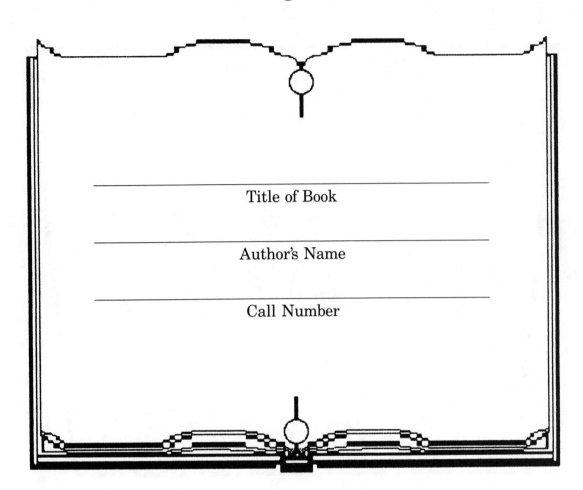

Title of Book

Author's Name

Call Number

NAME _____ DATE _____

BOOK REPORT MOBILE
Design #2

Draw a picture of your animal.
Name and color it.

NAME _____   DATE _____

BOOK REPORT MOBILE
Design #3

Write three interesting facts about your animal.

1. _____

_____

_____

_____

2. _____

_____

_____

_____

3. _____

_____

_____

_____

NAME _____   DATE _____

BOOK REPORT MOBILE
Design #4

The _____

My animal lives on the continent of _____.

Draw a picture of your animal's home:

NAME _____   GRADE _____

Research Report #8

ANIMAL MOBILE

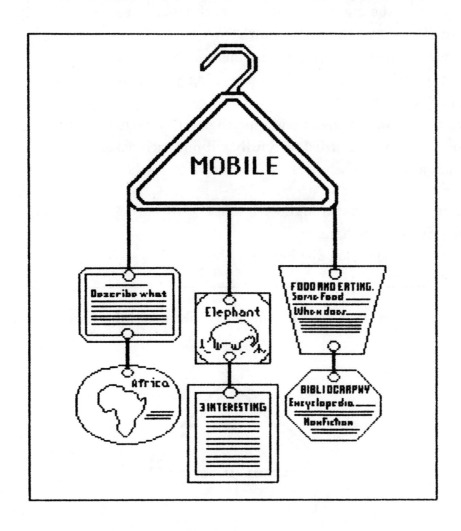

TEACHER _____   DATE _____

DIRECTIONS FOR MAKING AN ANIMAL MOBILE

Choose an animal to do your research report on. This report will be made into a mobile.

1. Check your library and classroom for books and other sources that will help you answer the questions found on each mobile design.
2. Read all you can about the animal you have chosen to research.
3. Jot down facts that will help you answer the questions.
4. Print or write as neatly as you can using your own sentences.
5. Color your designs.
6. Cut around your designs and glue them onto construction paper.
7. When the glue has dried, carefully cut out each design.
8. Punch a hole in each outline. You will need a hole at the bottom of three designs, too.
9. Tie strings or yarn through each hole.
10. Tie strings to the hanger.
11. Hang your mobile on display.

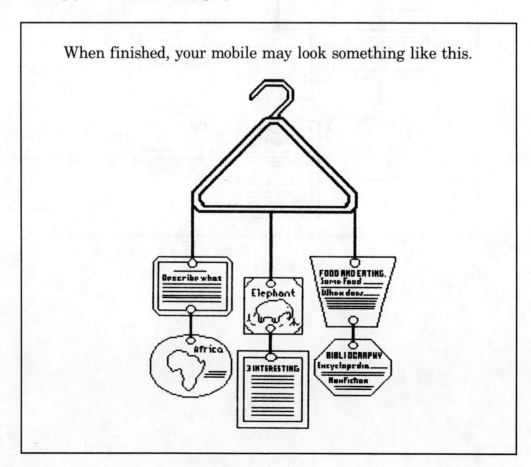

When finished, your mobile may look something like this.

ANIMAL MOBILE
Design #1

_____

Describe what your animal looks like when it is full grown.

_____

_____

_____

_____

_____

_____

Tell about your animal's body covering, color, distinguishing features, and size.

NAME _____   DATE _____

ANIMAL MOBILE
Design #2

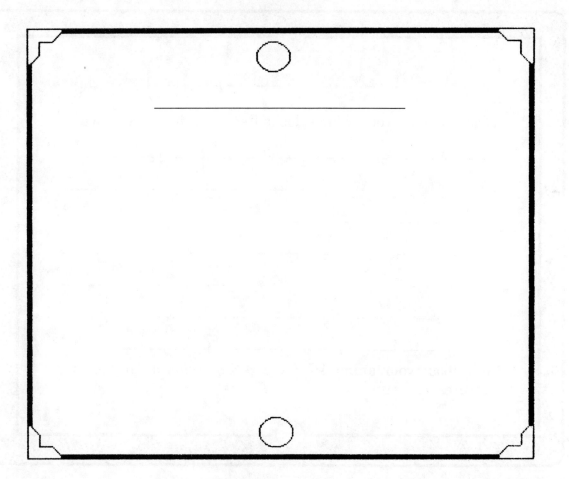

In the space above draw a picture of the animal you chose to do your research report on. Name and color your drawing.

NAME _____   **DATE** _____

ANIMAL MOBILE
Design #3

Food and eating habits of the _____

Some foods the _____ eats are:

_____

_____

When does your animal eat? _____

_____

_____

Tell about any strange eating habits your animal has. _____

_____

_____

_____

Draw some small pictures of your animal's food in the space
provided at the bottom of your mobile design.

ANIMAL MOBILE
Design #4

BIBLIOGRAPHY

Encyclopedia Title(s)   Vol.   Page(s)

_____   _____   _____

_____   _____   _____

Nonfiction Title(s)   Author   Page(s)

_____   _____   _____

_____   _____   _____

_____   _____   _____

Other Sources (Titles)   Type (Filmstrip, etc.)

_____   _____

_____   _____

_____   _____

NAME _____   DATE _____

ANIMAL MOBILE
Design #5

Write three interesting facts about your animal.

1. _____

_____

_____

_____

2. _____

_____

_____

_____

3. _____

_____

_____

_____

ANIMAL MOBILE
Design #6

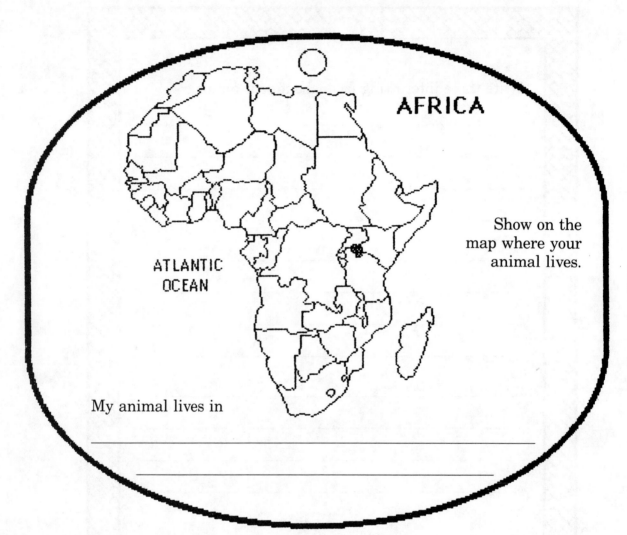

AFRICA

ATLANTIC
OCEAN

Show on the
map where your
animal lives.

My animal lives in

_____

_____

Substitute Pages

for

Research Report #8

NAME _____   DATE _____

ANIMAL MOBILE
Design #6

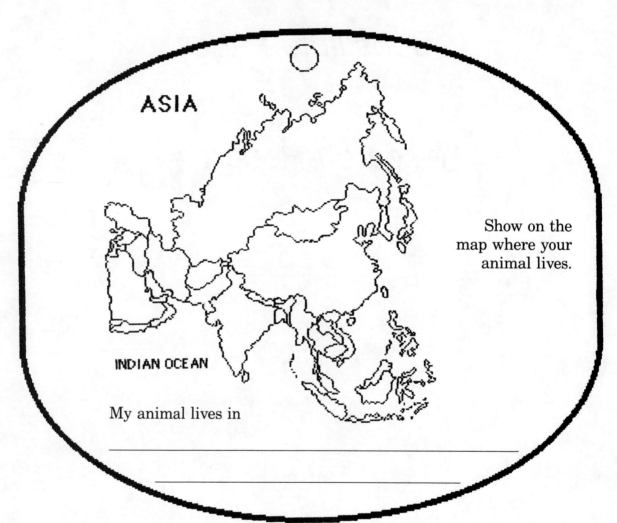

ASIA

Show on the
map where your
animal lives.

INDIAN OCEAN

My animal lives in

_____

_____

NAME _____   DATE _____

ANIMAL MOBILE
Design #6

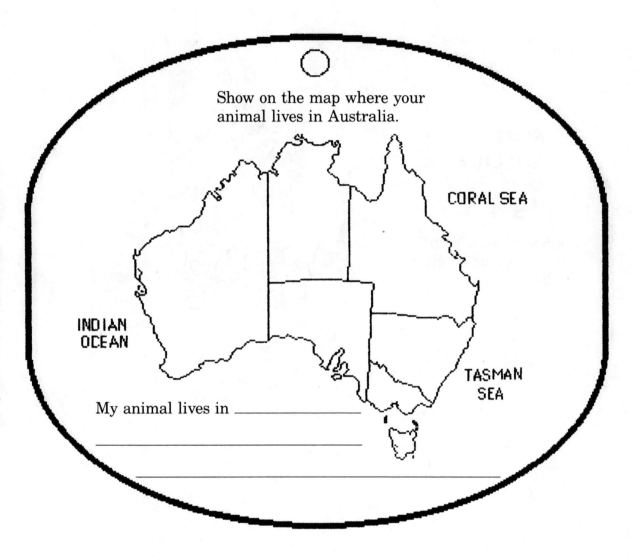

Show on the map where your
animal lives in Australia.

CORAL SEA

INDIAN
OCEAN

TASMAN
SEA

My animal lives in _____

_____

_____

NAME _____   DATE _____

ANIMAL MOBILE
Design #6

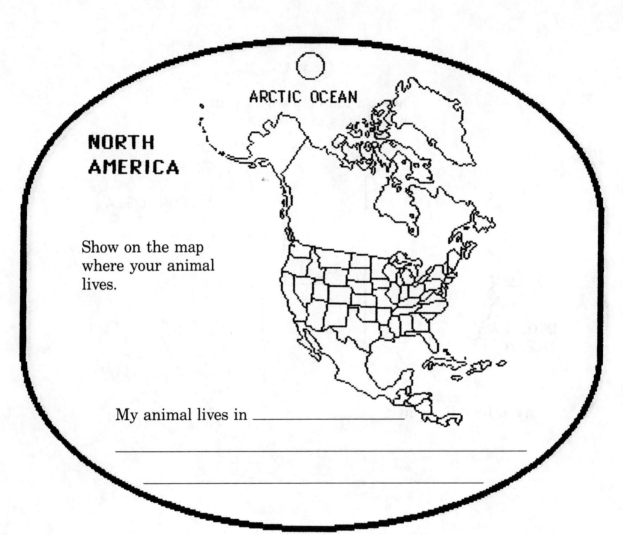

ARCTIC OCEAN

NORTH AMERICA

Show on the map where your animal lives.

My animal lives in _____

_____

_____

NAME _____   DATE _____

ANIMAL MOBILE
Design #6

Show on the map where your animal lives in South America.

My animal lives in _____

_____

_____

_____

NAME _____   GRADE _____

Research Report #9

PETS
AROUND
THE WORLD

TEACHER _____   DATE _____

NAME _____   **DATE** _____

THE PET I'M WRITING ABOUT

I chose the _____ .

Draw a picture of your favorite pet.

My pet's name is _____

NAME _____ **DATE** _____

INFORMATION ABOUT MY PET

What is the size of your pet when it is full grown? _____

_____

_____

_____

_____

What kinds of food does your pet like to eat? _____

_____

_____

_____

_____

Draw some pictures of your pet's favorite foods below. Name them.

NAME _____   DATE _____

ALL ABOUT MY PET'S HOME

Draw a picture of your pet's home.

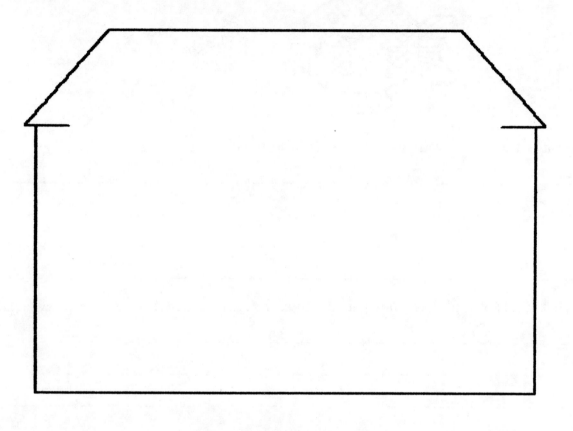

_____ home

Tell something special about your pet's home. _____

_____

_____

_____

_____

_____

_____

_____

Find a book in the library to help you.

NAME _____   DATE _____

MORE ABOUT MY PET

Does your pet like to play? If so, tell about it here. _____

_____

_____

_____

_____

Find a book in the library about your pet. Write down several more interesting facts

about it. _____

_____

_____

_____

_____

_____

NAME _____   GRADE _____

Research Report #10

ANIMAL DIARY

FIVE DAYS

IN MY

LIFE

TEACHER _____   DATE _____

NAME _____ DATE _____

DIRECTIONS FOR YOUR ANIMAL DIARY

1. Pretend that you are an animal for five days of your life.
2. Use reference sources from your library to help you gather true facts about the animal you have decided to be.
3. Or you may fill out your day-to-day diary by using the knowledge you already have about the animal.
4. Make sure that when you fill in the blanks with your own sentences, they make sense.
5. Your teacher or librarian will assist you if you need help.
6. HAVE FUN!

SO MANY CHOICES!

NAME _____   DATE _____

FIVE DAYS IN MY LIFE
Day One

Hi there! My name is _____

I am a _____ and I live in _____

_____

Here I am with my family.

```



```

When I woke up this morning I decided to eat _____

_____

Then I traveled _____

_____

On my way I _____

_____

Some other interesting things that I did today were _____

_____

_____

NAME _____   DATE _____

FIVE DAYS IN MY LIFE
Day Two

I woke up this morning _____

_____

As I continued traveling I _____

_____

+---+
| |
| Here is a picture of the countryside where I live: |
| |
| |
| |
| |
| |
| |
| |
+---+

Some of the animals I met today were _____

_____

I had a problem _____

_____

_____

I went to sleep about _____ after _____

_____

_____

NAME _____   DATE _____

FIVE DAYS IN MY LIFE
Day Three

I didn't sleep very well last night because _____

_____

_____

So I decided to _____

_____

_____

Then I _____

_____

Three exciting things that happened to me today were _____

_____

_____

_____

_____

I decided to go to bed early this evening and get a good night's rest because I must

_____

_____

_____

_____

This is where I slept during the night:

NAME _____   DATE _____

FIVE DAYS IN MY LIFE
Day Four

It was very _____ last night so I _____

_____

Since beginning this diary I have traveled _____

_____

_____

_____

Today I saw _____

_____

_____

Did you know that _____

are afraid of me because _____

_____

I really enjoyed my lunch today because I _____

_____

_____

The weather has turned _____

so I must _____

_____

This is what I had for lunch today:

NAME _____   DATE _____

FIVE DAYS IN MY LIFE
Day Five

When I awoke this morning I heard some strange noises. I went to see what they

were and found _____

_____

_____

Today I must _____

During the last five days I have traveled _____

_____

_____

All in all, the last five days have been _____

_____

_____

_____

The map below shows you where I traveled the last five days, where I slept each night, and the location of some of the interesting things I saw.

Activity Pages

to

Accompany Section II

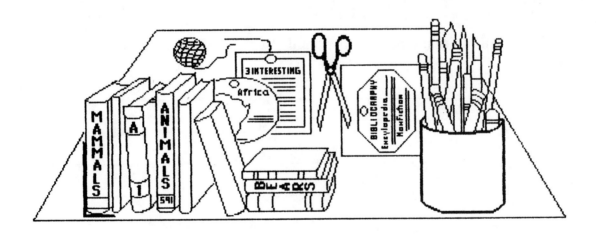

NAME _____   DATE _____

ANIMALS OF AFRICA

Vulture
Cheetah
Gorilla
Mamba
Ibis
Hyena
Flamingo
Crocodile
Lion
Gnu
Hippopotamus
Serval
Zebra
Elephant

Write the animals' names in alphabetical order as they would appear in the dictionary:

1. _____   8. _____

2. _____   9. _____

3. _____   10. _____

4. _____   11. _____

5. _____   12. _____

6. _____   13. _____

7. _____   14. _____

NAME _____   DATE _____

ANIMALS OF ASIA

WORD
LIST

Tiger
Gibbon
Caracal
Reindeer
Yak
Gaur
Onager
Leopard
Elephant
Lemming
Anoa
Ibex
Lynx
Monkey

Write the animals' names in alphabetical order as they would appear in the dictionary:

1. _____   8. _____

2. _____   9. _____

3. _____   10. _____

4. _____   11. _____

5. _____   12. _____

6. _____   13. _____

7. _____   14. _____

NAME _____   DATE _____

ANIMALS OF AUSTRALIA

Platypus
Echidna
Wombat
Fairy Penguin
Emu
Cuscus
Koala
Lyrebird
Dingo
Kangaroo
Bandicoot
Wallaby
Dugong
Kookaburra

Write the animals' names in alphabetical order as they would appear in the dictionary:

1. _____   8. _____

2. _____   9. _____

3. _____   10. _____

4. _____   11. _____

5. _____   12. _____

6. _____   13. _____

7. _____   14. _____

NAME _____   DATE _____

ANIMALS OF NORTH AMERICA

WORD LIST

Beaver
Skunk
Grizzly Bear
Porcupine
Buffalo
Eagle
Muskrat
Wolf
Rabbit
Seal
Coyote
Elk
Squirrel
Caribou

Write the animals' names in alphabetical order as they would appear in the dictionary:

1. _____   8. _____

2. _____   9. _____

3. _____   10. _____

4. _____   11. _____

5. _____   12. _____

6. _____   13. _____

7. _____   14. _____

NAME _____   DATE _____

ANIMALS OF SOUTH AMERICA

Peccary
Vicuna
Parrot
Guanaco
Cavy
Alpaca
Condor
Armadillo
Tapir
Iguana
Puma
Llama
Coati
Yapok

Write the animals' names in alphabetical order as they would appear in the dictionary:

1. _____   8. _____

2. _____   9. _____

3. _____   10. _____

4. _____   11. _____

5. _____   12. _____

6. _____   13. _____

7. _____   14. _____

NAME _____   **DATE** _____

PETS AROUND THE WORLD

WORD
LIST

Frog
Dog
Goldfish
Turtle
Cat
Rabbit
Hamster
Snake

Print your pet names in alphabetical order:

1. _____   5. _____

2. _____   6. _____

3. _____   7. _____

4. _____   8. _____

NAME _____   **DATE** _____

ANIMAL STORYBOOK REPORT

Visit your library. Pick out an animal story to read. Then fill in the information below.

Title of Book: _____

Author: _____

Illustrator: _____

Publisher: _____

Copyright Date: _____   Number of Pages _____

List four facts about your main character below.

Where did your story take place?

_____

1. _____   _____

_____   _____

2. _____   _____

_____   Is your story fiction or nonfiction?

3. _____   _____ How do you know?

_____   _____

4. _____   _____

_____

In the space below tell about your favorite part of the story.

Draw a picture of one of the characters in your story.

_____

_____

_____

_____

NAME _____   DATE _____

ANY PET IN THE WORLD

If you could have any animal in the world for a pet, what would it be?

_____

Draw a picture of it below.

WANTED

My pet's name is _____

Write a story about your new pet. What does it look like? Can it do anything special? If you need more space to write, use the back of this sheet.

_____

_____

_____

_____

_____

_____

_____

_____

_____

AFRICAN ANIMAL BOOKMARK

Choose one nonfiction book on African animals. After you have read it, fill in the information below. Then color and cut out your bookmark. Share it with a friend.

QUIT 'LION' AROUND
READ

_____
Title of Book

_____
Author's Name

You should read this
book because _____
_____
_____
_____
_____
_____
_____
_____

Glue your bookmark
on heavier paper or
have it laminated.

ASIAN ANIMAL BOOKMARK

Choose one nonfiction book to read about Asian animals. After you have read it, fill in the information below. Then color your bookmark and cut it out. Share it with a friend.

R - R - R - R - R

READ

_____
Title of Book

_____
Author's Name

**Reasons to read this
book are:** _____
_____
_____
_____
_____
_____
_____
_____
_____

Glue your bookmark
on heavier paper or
have it laminated.

NAME _____   DATE _____

AUSTRALIAN ANIMAL BOOKMARK

Choose one nonfiction book to read about the animals of Australia. After you have read it, fill in the information below. Then color your bookmark and cut it out. Share it with a friend.

SHARE WITH A FRIEND

_____
Title of Book
_____
Author's Name
Three facts I found in this book were :

_____
_____
_____
_____
_____
_____
_____
_____
_____

Glue your bookmark on heavier paper or have it laminated.

NAME _____ DATE _____

NORTH AMERICAN ANIMAL BOOKMARK

Choose one nonfiction book to read about the animals of North America. After you have read it, fill in the information below. Then color your bookmark and cut it out. Share it with a friend.

SEAL OF APPROVAL

_____
Title of Book

_____
Author's Name
Why I liked this book
_____
_____
_____
_____
_____
_____
_____
_____
_____

Glue your bookmark on heavier paper or have it laminated.

NAME _____   DATE _____

SOUTH AMERICAN ANIMAL BOOKMARK

Choose one nonfiction book about South American animals. After you have read it, fill in the information below. Then color your bookmark and cut it out. Share it with a friend.

READ ABOUT ANIMALS
OF SOUTH AMERICA

_____
Title of Book

_____
Author's Name
Why I liked this book
_____
_____
_____
_____
_____
_____
_____
_____

Glue your bookmark
on heavier paper or
have it laminated.

PET BOOKMARK

Choose one book about a pet. After you have read it, answer the question on the bookmark below. Then color your book mark and cut it out. Share it with a friend.

WILD HORSES COULDN'T PULL ME AWAY

_____

Title of Book

_____

Author's Name

I liked this book because _____

_____

_____

_____

_____

_____

_____

Glue your bookmark on heavier paper or have it laminated.

NAME _____ DATE _____

ANIMALS AND THE CONTINENTS THEY LIVE ON

Name one continent that each of these animals lives on. Use encyclopedias from your resource center to help you. Give your source and page number.

I am an anteater.
I am also called
an _____

ANIMAL	CONTINENT	SOURCE	PAGE
Aardvark	_____	_____	_____
Bettong	_____	_____	_____
Civet	_____	_____	_____
Dugong	_____	_____	_____
Elk	_____	_____	_____
Gnu	_____	_____	_____
Jaguar	_____	_____	_____
Lemur	_____	_____	_____
Mulgara	_____	_____	_____
Oryx	_____	_____	_____
Vervet	_____	_____	_____
Wapiti	_____	_____	_____
Yak	_____	_____	_____

What continent
do I live on?

_____

©1987 by The Center for Applied Research in Education, Inc.

NAME _____ **DATE** _____

MAMMALS OF AFRICA

WORD LIST

Ape
Dromedary
Eland
Elephants
Fox
Giraffes
Hippopotamus
Lions
Rhinoceros
Zebra

ACROSS

1. Another name for chimpanzee

   is _____ .

4. _____ usually live in a pride.

7. An African _____ has two horns.

8. A fennec is a desert _____ .

9. We can tell a _____ by its stripes.

10. _____ live in Africa and Asia.

DOWN

2. _____ means "river horse."

3. The _____ is Africa's largest antelope.

5. _____ are known for their long neck and legs.

6. A _____ is a kind of camel.

NAME _____   DATE _____

MAMMALS OF ASIA

WORD LIST

Buffalo
Elephant
Gibbons
Leopard
Pandas
Tarsier
Tiger
Yak

ACROSS

1. The _____ , which lives in Tibet, looks something like a buffalo.

4. The _____ can run, jump, climb trees, and swim across rivers.

7. The water _____ of Southeast Asia is used for work.

8. The _____ is about six inches long with a ten-inch tail.

DOWN

2. The Indian _____ is much smaller than its African look-alike.

3. Giant _____ love to eat bamboo shoots.

5. _____ are the smallest of the ape family.

6. The Bengal _____ is a fierce animal.

NAME _____   DATE _____

MAMMALS OF AUSTRALIA

WORD LIST

Anteater
Bandicoots
Cuscus
Dingo
Joey
Kangaroo
Koala
Platypus
Pouch
Wombat

ACROSS

5. An echidna is also called spiny

   _____ .

7. A marsupial is a mammal that carries its young in a _____ .

9. The _____ bear lives in a tree and is sometimes called a teddy bear.

10. Most _____ are rabbit-sized or smaller.

DOWN

1. The _____ has a duck-like bill and webbed feet.

2. A baby kangaroo is called

   a _____ .

3. The _____ is a wild dog.

4. The _____ jumps in leaps and bounds.

6. At first sight a _____ looks like a small bear or marmot.

8. The _____ usually feeds and nests alone.

NAME _____   DATE _____

MAMMALS OF NORTH AMERICA

WORD LIST

Bats
Beaver
Bison
Cub
Deer
Fox
Grizzly
Moose
Porcupine
Prairie
Raccoon
Seals
Skunks
Squirrel

ACROSS

1. Vampire _____ hang upside down while sleeping.

3. A _____ dog looks like a ground squirrel.

4. A _____ sometimes washes its food in water.

5. Striped _____ can make interesting pets.

8. A baby bear is called a _____ .

10. _____ have large antlers.

12. _____ bears live in the Rockies.

DOWN

1. A _____ builds its home in a pond.

2. _____ eat fish, squid, and octopus.

3. A _____ has many quills.

6. One kind of _____ seems to fly from tree to tree.

7. _____ is another word for buffalo.

9. Some _____ get their name from their white tail.

11. A _____ can be gray, red, or white in color.

NAME _____   DATE _____

MAMMALS OF SOUTH AMERICA

WORD LIST

Anteater
Armadillo
Chinchilla
Jaguar
Llama
Peccary
Puma
Sloth
Tapir
Yapok

ACROSS

1. The world's laziest animal is called a _____ .

3. The hoglike _____ can grow as large as a pony.

5. A dangerous South American cat is called a _____ .

6. The _____ has beautiful warm fur.

8. A _____ looks a bit like a tiny wild boar.

9. A giant _____ is a strange-looking creature with a long snout and tongue.

DOWN

2. The guanaco, alpaca, and vicuna are related to the _____ .

4. The _____ has bony plates of armor.

7. A water opossum is also called a _____ .

8. The _____ is called the lion of South America.

NAME _____   **DATE** _____

PETS AROUND THE WORLD

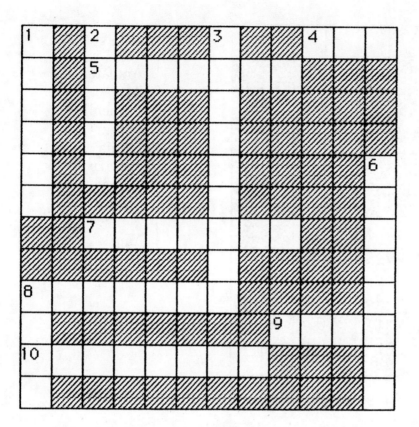

WORD LIST

Animals
Cat
Goldfish
Hamsters
Horses
Kittens
Mice
Parakeets
Pigs
Puppies
Water

ACROSS

4. A full-grown kitten is called a

_____ .

5. Gerbils are really desert _____ .

7. _____ love to play with a ball of yarn.

8. _____ like to chew bones.

9. _____ really like cheese.

10. You feed your _____ once a day.

DOWN

1. Some boys and girls love to ride

_____ .

2. Some pets need _____ bottles in their cages.

3. _____ will climb onto your finger when they get to know you.

6. _____ need more fresh vegetables than most rodents.

8. Guinea _____ cannot jump.

NAME _____   DATE _____

FAVORITE ANIMAL POEM

Choose some poetry books about animals to read. Then write one of your favorite poems below.

_____
Title
_____
_____
_____
_____
_____
_____
_____
_____
_____
_____
_____
_____

Who is the author of your poem? _____

Tell why you enjoyed the poem. _____

_____

_____

_____

_____

MEMORIZE YOUR POEM AND SAY IT TO A FRIEND.

NAME _____   DATE _____

MY FAVORITE WILD ANIMAL

Do some research in your library or classroom. Write the answers to these questions.

My favorite wild animal is the _____

I like this animal because _____

_____

_____

_____

_____

_____

Draw a picture of your favorite wild animal.

_____
NAME

NAME _____   DATE _____

How many words can you make from the word ELEPHANT?

2- and 3-letter words   4-letter words   Words with more than 4 letters

_____   _____   _____
_____   _____   _____
_____   _____   _____
_____   _____   _____
_____   _____   _____
_____   _____   _____
_____   _____   _____
_____   _____   _____
_____   _____   _____
_____   _____   _____
_____   _____   _____
_____   _____   _____
_____   _____   _____
_____   _____   _____

Number of words   Number of words   Number of words

_____   _____   _____

Use your dictionary to check your spelling before showing this page to your teacher or librarian.

Have a contest with your friends or the class to see who can make the most words.

NAME _____   DATE _____

PLANNING A DIORAMA

Choose a book to read. It may be on a topic that your librarian or your teacher gives you or you may choose your own. After you have read your book, make a diorama to show your favorite part of the story. A diorama is a three-dimensional miniature scene using a painted background and model figures.

Look at the diorama below to give you an idea.

In order to make a diorama you will need:

1 shoe box	pencil crayons
drawing paper	crayons or markers
glue	construction paper
scissors	paint and paintbrush
pencil	eraser
ruler	other assorted items

Some boys and girls also like to use modeling clay, twigs for trees, etc., to make their dioramas more realistic.

Read the next page for the rest of the instructions.

HAVE FUN AND BE CREATIVE!

NAME _____   DATE _____

MAKING A DIORAMA

The following suggestions will assist you in making a diorama, but don't forget to use your own ideas also.

1. Cover the outside of your box with paper or paint it.

2. Paint in a background for your diorama. Make sure it suits the rest of your plans. For instance, you may paint trees, mountains, and a river if your story takes place in the wilderness or paint the background like the inside of a house if it is an indoor scene.

3. Make models, then draw and color all the things you wish to add to your diorama. You might add animals, people, cars, trees, or anything else.

4. Make a tab on all your drawings before cutting them out. Look at the samples below for help.

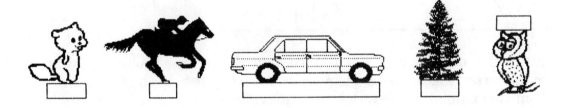

5. Fold the tabs under and put glue on them before placing them.

6. If you made models put them in place.

7. When your diorama is completed fill in the label below. Cut it out and glue it on the top or side of the box.

Title of Book: _____
Author: _____ No. of Pages_____
I chose a scene about _____
_____
_____
_____
_____
By _____ Gr. ____ Date: _____

NAME _____   DATE _____

MIX-UP MANIA: ANIMALS OF AFRICA

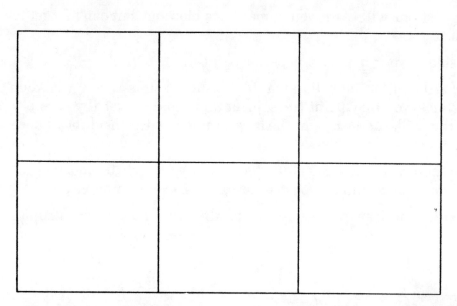

What AFRICAN
animal is this?

_____

©1987 by The Center for Applied Research in Education, Inc.

   This mother and her baby are all mixed up. Cut out the squares below and glue them in the correct places above. Then use your library to help you find some information about this animal. Write at least three facts here. My mixed-up animals are:

_____

1. _____

2. _____

3. _____

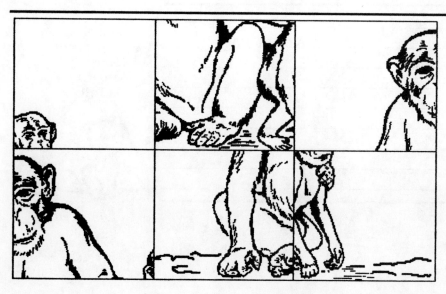

Color your picture
when you're finished.

NAME _____   DATE _____

MIX-UP MANIA: ANIMALS OF ASIA

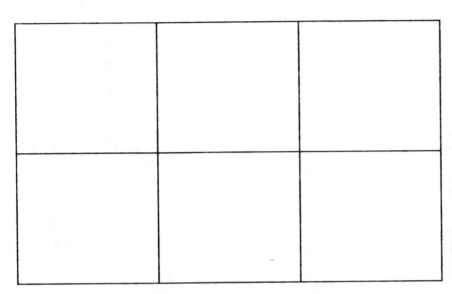

What ASIAN
animal is this?

_____

This mother and her baby are all mixed up. Cut out the squares below and glue them in the correct places above. Then use your library to help you find some information about this animal. Write at least three facts here. My mixed-up animals are:

_____

1. _____

2. _____

3. _____

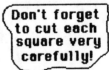

Color your picture
when you're finished.

NAME _____ DATE _____

MIX-UP MANIA: ANIMALS OF AUSTRALIA

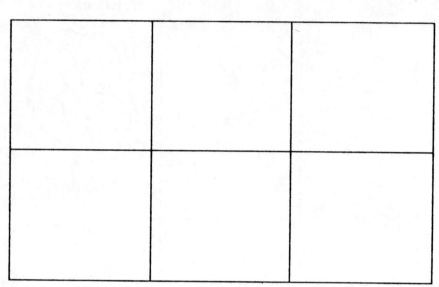

What AUSTRALIAN animal is this?

©1987 by The Center for Applied Research in Education, Inc.

This mother and her baby are all mixed up. Cut out the squares below and glue them in the correct places above. Then use your library to help you find some information about this animal. Write at least three facts here. My mixed-up animals are:

_____

1. _____

2. _____

3. _____

Color your picture when you're finished.

NAME _____ **DATE** _____

MIX-UP MANIA: ANIMALS OF NORTH AMERICA

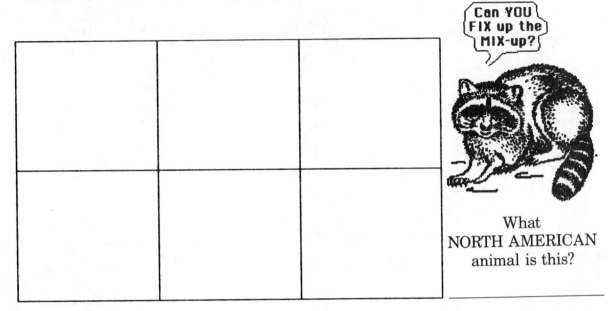

What
NORTH AMERICAN
animal is this?

This mother and her baby are all mixed up. Cut out the squares below and glue them in the correct places above. Then use your library to help you find some information about this animal. Write at least three facts here. My mixed-up animals are:

_____

1. _____

2. _____

3. _____

Color your picture
when you're finished.

NAME _____   DATE _____

MIX-UP MANIA: ANIMALS OF SOUTH AMERICA

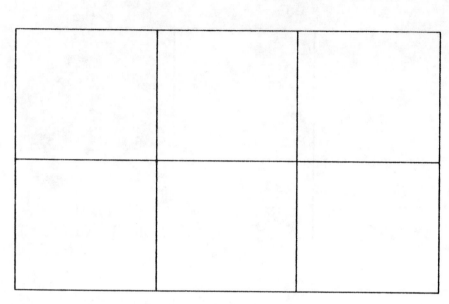

Can YOU FIX up the MIX-up?

What
SOUTH AMERICAN
animal is this?

This mother and her baby are all mixed up. Cut out the squares below and glue them in the correct places above. Then use your library to help you find some information about this animal. Write at least three facts here. My mixed-up animals are:

_____

1. _____

2. _____

3. _____

Don't forget to cut each square very carefully!

Color your picture
when you're finished.

NAME _____   DATE _____

MIX-UP MANIA: PETS AROUND THE WORLD

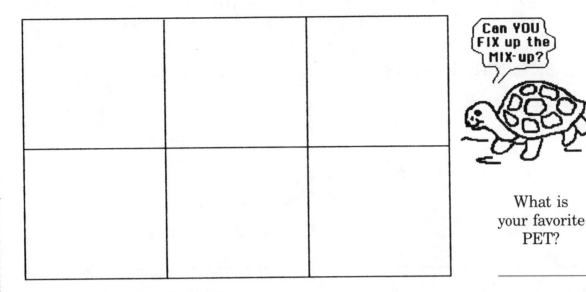

Can YOU FIX up the MIX-up?

What is
your favorite
PET?

_____

This mother and her baby are all mixed up. Cut out the squares below and glue them in the correct places above. Then write a short story about this favorite pet below:

_____

_____

_____

_____

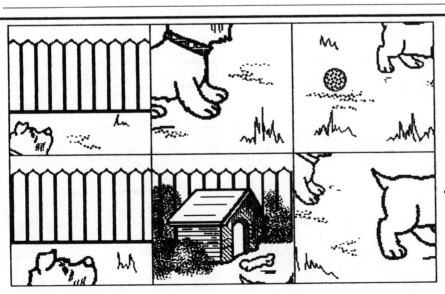

Don't forget to cut each square very carefully!

Color your picture
when you're finished.

II-33

NAME _____ DATE _____

REGIONS WHERE ANIMALS LIVE

Use reference sources from your library and list five animals that live in these special places.

ANTARCTIC REGIONS
1. ___
2. ___
3. ___
4. ___
5. ___

ARCTIC REGIONS
1. ___
2. ___
3. ___
4. ___
5. ___

DESERT REGIONS
1. ___
2. ___
3. ___
4. ___
5. ___

FOREST REGIONS
1. ___
2. ___
3. ___
4. ___
5. ___

MOUNTAIN REGIONS
1. ___
2. ___
3. ___
4. ___
5. ___

PRAIRIE REGIONS
1. ___
2. ___
3. ___
4. ___
5. ___

©1987 by The Center for Applied Research in Education, Inc.

NAME _____   DATE _____

FIND THE AFRICAN MAMMALS

Look for the African mammals listed at the bottom of this sheet. Be careful! The words can be found forward, backward, horizontally, vertically, and diagonally.

T	V	A	D	O	K	A	P	I	C	N	R
N	I	R	J	R	H	R	T	S	F	O	N
A	K	H	T	H	E	E	R	E	O	I	L
H	M	F	O	I	H	R	I	P	R	L	A
P	G	E	T	N	P	D	S	O	N	K	P
E	R	N	A	O	P	O	I	L	M	O	E
L	E	N	R	C	C	A	M	E	L	H	N
E	L	E	O	E	A	H	K	T	R	E	Y
W	S	C	P	R	L	K	O	N	U	M	E
H	I	P	P	O	P	O	T	A	M	U	S
O	G	D	R	S	K	H	F	D	U	D	P
S	Z	E	B	R	A	R	T	E	P	A	I

When you find the animal, fill in the missing letter in the word list:

WORD LIST

A __ TELOPE   HIPPOPOTA __ US

A __ E   L __ ON

CAM __ L   OK __ PI

ELEP __ ANT   RHINO __ EROS

FE __ NEC   Z __ BRA

Elephant

NAME _____   DATE _____

FIND THE ASIAN MAMMALS

Look for the Asian mammals listed at the bottom of this sheet. Be careful! The words can be found forward, backward, horizontally, vertically, and diagonally.

A	L	R	H	I	N	O	C	E	R	O	S
N	E	P	H	S	O	L	E	M	A	C	K
O	R	O	E	E	L	A	C	B	K	L	M
A	M	A	P	L	E	T	R	O	C	B	F
F	O	R	L	E	S	H	A	R	P	C	E
K	P	C	K	P	T	T	S	A	B	I	S
A	H	B	A	H	P	I	P	N	H	H	O
Y	K	N	C	A	R	G	T	G	I	T	O
D	D	M	D	N	A	E	E	U	J	S	G
A	T	M	P	T	C	R	L	T	K	A	N
K	R	K	H	P	I	N	K	A	M	R	O
L	E	O	P	A	R	D	N	N	O	P	M

When you find the animal, fill in the missing letter in the word list:

WORD LIST

A __ OA   ORA __ GUTAN

CAM __ L   PA __ DA

ELE __ HANT   R __ INOCEROS

L __ OPARD   TI __ ER

MONG __ OSE   Y __ K

Camel

NAME _____   DATE _____

FIND THE AUSTRALIAN MAMMALS

Look for the Australian mammals listed at the bottom of this sheet. Be careful!
The words can be found forward, backward, horizontally, vertically, and diagonally.

```
P   R   S   O   O   R   A   G   N   A   K   T
R   A   N   C   B   K   L   A   T   E   B   L
B   T   E   P   S   U   P   Y   T   A   L   P
A   C   C   C   M   N   O   E   L   P   R   A
N   R   H   T   I   R   A   W   O   K   K   W
D   H   I   L   D   E   A   Y   S   A   D   O
I   P   D   A   I   N   P   K   R   P   M   M
C   N   N   P   N   L   O   E   O   S   T   B
O   T   A   R   G   R   R   T   A   A   E   A
O   O   T   S   O   H   C   K   L   A   L   T
T   L   W   A   L   L   A   B   Y   B   C   A
F   R   E   T   N   L   S   U   C   S   U   C
```

When you find the animal, fill in the missing letter in the word list:

```
+-----------------------------------------+
|              WORD LIST                  |
|                                         |
|  BANDIC __OT     KANGAR __ O            |
|                                         |
|  CUSC __ S       K __ ALA              |
|                                         |
|  DI __ GO        P __ ATYPUS           |
|                                         |
|  E __ HIDNA      WALL __ BY            |
|                                         |
|  KO __ ARI       WO __ BAT             |
+-----------------------------------------+
```

Kangaroo

NAME _____   DATE _____

FIND THE NORTH AMERICAN MAMMALS

Look for the North American mammals listed at the bottom of this sheet. Be careful! The words can be found forward, backward, horizontally, vertically, and diagonally.

E	A	A	T	I	B	B	A	R	B	B	C
N	C	D	S	E	E	E	S	O	O	M	D
I	E	E	Q	F	A	D	C	C	B	M	R
P	O	C	U	U	A	R	R	L	B	S	R
U	S	L	I	D	B	A	D	G	E	R	E
C	E	E	R	M	R	A	B	F	A	V	S
R	A	C	R	A	E	B	R	W	V	O	E
O	L	D	E	E	E	P	E	R	E	A	F
P	R	H	L	U	D	W	X	M	R	R	L
A	C	L	P	S	T	A	E	O	S	L	O
C	H	I	P	M	U	N	K	T	F	S	W
D	R	M	X	O	S	T	A	R	W	V	L

When you find the animal, fill in the missing letter in the word list:

WORD LIST

B __ DGER   MO __ SE

BE __ R   PORCU __ INE

BEA __ ER   RA __ BIT

CHIPM __ NK   R __ T

D __ ER   S __ AL

F __ X   SQUI __ REL

M __ CE   WO __ F

moose

©1987 by The Center for Applied Research in Education, Inc.

NAME _____   DATE _____

FIND THE SOUTH AMERICAN MAMMALS

Look for the South American mammals listed at the bottom of this sheet. Be careful! The words can be found forward, backward, horizontally, vertically, and diagonally.

```
J  P  S  L  O  T  H  A  S  R  L  T
B  A  G  S  O  M  L  R  H  I  P  L
C  L  G  K  E  L  S  M  R  P  S  L
D  H  H  U  M  G  H  A  P  A  T  A
P  E  C  C  A  R  Y  D  M  T  A  M
A  R  P  C  R  R  T  I  O  L  E  A
C  H  I  N  C  H  I  L  L  A  M  E
L  P  L  N  H  G  P  L  T  E  C  D
M  A  R  N  T  B  R  O  A  B  B  E
T  E  S  O  M  R  A  M  B  M  M  X
R  S  E  M  T  S  Y  M  S  P  U  T
O  C  A  N  A  U  G  E  G  T  Y  P
```

When you find the animal, fill in the missing letter in the word list:

+-------------------------------------+
| WORD LIST |
| |
| ARMADI __ LO   MARMO __ ET |
| |
| C __ INCHILLA   PE __ CARY |
| |
| GUA __ ACO   P __ MA |
| |
| JAG __ AR   SLO __ H |
| |
| LL __ MA   TAP __ R |
+-------------------------------------+

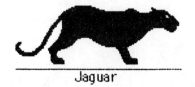
Jaguar

NAME _____   **DATE** _____

FIND THE PETS

Look for the pets listed at the bottom of this sheet. Be careful! The words can be found forward, backward, horizontally, vertically, and diagonally.

P	O	R	L	T	P	S	N	E	T	A	C
U	E	L	I	Z	A	R	D	T	O	A	C
P	L	N	L	C	R	M	C	U	R	P	R
P	T	E	R	K	A	Z	P	E	L	T	A
I	R	T	M	H	K	S	U	O	N	L	B
E	U	H	N	S	E	A	Z	T	E	H	B
S	T	L	G	L	E	T	E	K	T	K	I
P	N	O	S	S	T	A	R	R	T	M	T
T	D	F	X	P	N	L	Z	M	I	N	C
R	D	A	O	T	L	R	L	O	K	S	L
I	L	H	K	X	I	Z	X	R	N	P	A
K	S	N	A	K	E	O	S	G	O	R	F

When you find the animal, fill in the missing letter in the word list:

WORD LIST

C __ T   P __ PPIES

DO __ S   RA __ BIT

FROG __   RA __ S

K __ TTEN   SNA __ E

L __ ZARD   T __ AD

PAR __ KEET   TU __ TLE

Rabbit

LANDS AND PEOPLE OF THE WORLD

TO THE TEACHER

Section III contains the following five reports that can be used by individuals, small groups, or the entire class. Project instructions are included with each report.

- Research Report #11, "Countries Around the World," can be used by students to research the continents of Africa, Asia, Australia, Europe, North America, and South America. It is suitable for grades 3 and 4.

- Research Report #12, "I Like My Place Best," is useful for beginners or more experienced researchers interested in finding out more about the state or province in which they live. This report is suitable for grades 2–4.

- Research Report #13, "People Who Live at Our House," gives beginning researchers an opportunity to report on themselves and their family. It is suitable for grades 1–3.

- Research Report #14, "Travel Talk," gives more experienced students practice in using travel guides, brochures, and other reference sources in order to assist them in pretending to be a travel agent. They must plan a five-day itinerary for a bus tour through part of a country found on one of the continents in the world. This project is suitable for grade 4.

- Research Report #15, "Famous People Around the World," gives students a chance to report on an important person. They may read a book or use other reference sources to assist them in answering the questions presented in the report. This report is suitable for grades 2–4.

The activity pages that follow the research reports enhance the learning experiences of the students involved. Topics related to map making, using the atlas, learning geographical facts and terms, and using a variety of research resources in order to learn more about a country will provide additional challenge and fun.

NAME _____   GRADE _____

Research Report #11

COUNTRIES AROUND THE WORLD

TEACHER _____   DATE _____

NAME _____   DATE _____

PROJECT INSTRUCTIONS

1. Choose a country found on one of our continents. It may be one suggested by your teacher or librarian or you may have picked out your own.

2. If you had your own choice, look at maps, your globe, and geography books to help you decide.

3. After you have decided on your country, go to the card catalog in your library resource center and look up your country. Choose at least one nonfiction book to use. Check your encyclopedias, geography reference sets, and other sources as well, for additional information. Remember, there may be more than one country on the continent you choose.

4. Ask your teacher or librarian for assistance if you need help.

5. Read all about the country you have chosen. Then close your books and answer the questions found in the report. Jot down your facts in your own words on note paper. Or if you want to be really organized, use the small cards found in Research Report #4, "Note-Taking Knacks." (Ask your teacher or librarian to make copies of these for you.) Write or print the answers to the questions in your own sentences. Do not copy word-for-word from your reference sources.

Some of the questions in your research project will not require cards, so read your project questions carefully before you start working on them.

6. Your teacher or librarian may wish you to include your own title page, table of contents page, and bibliography page before handing in your report. If so, he or she will explain what you must do.

Don't forget sources such as films, filmstrips, magazines, pamphlets, and television. They may give you information about your country, too.

NAME _____   DATE _____

THE COUNTRY I'M WRITING ABOUT

I chose the country of _____

Draw a map of your country below. Show the <u>main cities</u> and <u>main lakes and rivers</u>. Be sure to print neatly.

NAME _____   DATE _____

THINGS I SHOULD KNOW ABOUT _____

1. _____ is found on the continent of _____

2. What is the size of your country? _____

   _____

   _____

3. What is the population?

   _____

4. What is the main language(s) spoken? _____

   _____

5. Name several nationalities of people that live there:

   _____

   _____

6. In the space below, draw a picture to show one kind of home the people of this country live in. If the home has a special name, print it under your drawing.

NAME _____   DATE _____

THE COUNTRY'S ATTRACTIONS

What are the major tourist attractions in your country?

_____

_____

_____

_____

_____

Draw a picture of several of them below. Name them.

Name several historical sites. _____

_____

_____

_____

Draw pictures of three historical sites below. Name them.

THE COUNTRY'S FLOWERS

Draw a picture of your country's floral emblem. Name it.

Name several other flowers that grow in this country.

_____

_____

_____

_____

Draw pictures of them below:

NAME _____   DATE _____

THE COUNTRY'S FOOD SOURCES
AND TRANSPORTATION

What kinds of food are eaten by the people in the country you are researching?

_____

_____

_____

Draw pictures below. Name each kind of food.

What kinds of transportation do the people use?

_____

_____

_____

_____

Draw several pictures to show the way they travel.

NAME _____   **DATE** _____

THE COUNTRY'S ANIMALS

Draw a picture of an animal that lives in this country. Name the animal.

My animal is the _____

Write the names of several other animals that live there.

_____

_____

Draw pictures of them, also. Color and name your animals.

NAME _____   DATE _____

THE COUNTRY'S BIRDS

Draw a picture of the national bird. Name it.

The national bird is the _____

Tell about the national bird in three or four sentences.

_____

_____

_____

_____

_____

Write the names of several other birds that live in this country.

_____

_____

NAME _____   DATE _____

THE COUNTRY'S FLAG AND INDUSTRY

Draw a picture of the national flag and color it.

Tell about the national flag in three or four sentences.

_____

_____

_____

_____

_____

_____

List three products grown in this country.

_____   _____   _____

What is the major industry in this country?_____

_____

_____

Ask your teacher or librarian for help, if you need assistance.

NAME _____   DATE _____

MORE ABOUT THE COUNTRY I CHOSE

Tell three ways in which this country is similar to where you live.

1. _____

_____

2. _____

_____

3. _____

_____

Tell three ways in which this country is different from where you live.

1. _____

_____

2. _____

_____

3. _____

_____

What did you like best about the country you found your information on? Tell why.

_____

_____

_____

_____

Would you like to live in the country you studied about? Tell why.

_____

_____

_____

_____

NAME _____ GRADE _____

Research Report #12

I LIKE
MY PLACE
BEST

THERE'S NO PLACE LIKE HOME

TEACHER _____ DATE _____

NAME _____   DATE _____

PROJECT INSTRUCTIONS

This research report is to be done on the state or province in which you live.

1. Check your library or classroom for maps, an encyclopedia, and a geography book to help you.

2. You can answer some questions in this report just by using your own knowledge about the place you live in.

3. Ask your teacher or librarian for help if you need assistance.

4. Write or print as neatly as you can and draw and color your pictures carefully.

ALWAYS TRY TO DO YOUR BEST!

NAME _____   **DATE** _____

WHERE I LIVE

I live in the _____ of _____

My country is _____

I live on the continent of _____

My address is:

_____

_____

_____

    In the space below, draw an outline map of your state or province. Show the state or provincial capital, the largest river, and the place where you live.

NAME _____   **DATE** _____

THE FLOWER AND THE FLAG

Draw a picture of your state or provincial flower. Name and color it.

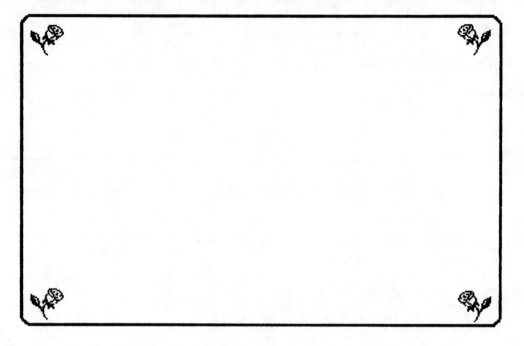

My flower is called the _____

Draw a picture of your state or provincial flag. Color it.

NAME _____   DATE _____

SUMMER SPORTS

What are the summer sports played where you live?

_____

_____

_____

Draw several pictures to show them. Name and color your drawings.

What is your favorite summer sport?

_____

Draw a picture of it below.

12-5

NAME _____   DATE _____

WINTER SPORTS

What are the winter sports played where you live?

_____

_____

_____

Draw several pictures to show them. Name and color your drawings.

What is your favorite winter sport?

_____

Draw a picture of it below.

NAME _____   DATE _____

THE DIFFERENT LANDSCAPES

Each state or province has its own special scenery or countryside. Draw three pictures below to show the different landscapes in the area where you live. Write a sentence about each.

1. _____

_____

2. _____

_____

3. _____

_____

NAME _____   GRADE _____

Research Report #13

PEOPLE WHO LIVE AT OUR HOUSE

TEACHER _____   DATE _____

NAME _____   **DATE** _____

A PICTURE OF ME

My name is _____

I live at _____

_____

_____

THIS IS A PICTURE OF ME

NAME _____   **DATE** _____

A PICTURE OF MY FAMILY

I live with _____

_____

_____

_____

HERE IS A PICTURE OF MY FAMILY

Some of my best friends are _____

_____

_____

SOME FACTS ABOUT MYSELF

List some of your favorite foods.

_____

_____

_____

_____

_____

Draw some pictures. Name and color the foods.

What are some chores you do around your house to help your family? Tell about them here.

_____

_____

_____

_____

_____

_____

NAME _____   **DATE** _____

MY HOUSE

Describe the kind of house you live in.

_____

_____

_____

_____

_____

_____

_____

_____

_____

Draw a picture of your home. Color it.

NAME _____   DATE _____

MY LIKES AND DISLIKES

What are three things you really like to do? Write a sentence about each one:

1. _____

_____

2. _____

_____

3. _____

_____

Draw a picture of your favorite pastime.

What are three things you dislike very much? Write a sentence about each one:

1. _____

_____

2. _____

_____

3. _____

_____

NAME _____   DATE _____

THINGS MY FAMILY DOES TOGETHER

Draw pictures to show some of the things your family does together. Name each picture and color it.

TRAVEL TALK

TRAVEL TOURS

NAME _____   DATE _____

PROJECT INSTRUCTIONS

1. Pretend that you are a travel agent. You must plan an itinerary for a five-day bus tour through part of a country found on one of the continents in the world.

2. Decide on a continent, and then on the part of that continent that you will tour.

3. Use maps, encyclopedias, travel brochures, and other reference sources to help you plan the trip.

4. Follow this booklet. Answer the questions about the part of the country you will be traveling in very carefully. You want your passengers to be well-informed before they leave home.

5. For the pages in this booklet named Day 1–Day 5, use lined paper underneath when printing or writing anything on them. This will keep your pages much neater.

6. Design your own tour booklet cover if you wish, after you have completed the project.

HAVE FUN PLANNING THIS TRIP!

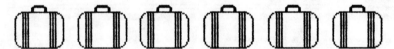

NAME _____   DATE _____

THE ROUTE WE'LL BE TAKING

This is a map of _____ where the tour takes place. The main cities and some points of interest are marked on it. The route we will be following from Day 1–Day 5 is shown in red.

14-3

NAME _____ DATE _____

THINGS I SHOULD KNOW FOR THE TRIP

This trip begins in _____

and ends in _____

WHAT I SHOULD KNOW BEFORE LEAVING:

Total price of the trip: _____

This price includes: _____

_____

_____

_____

_____

_____

_____

Currency I will use: _____

_____

Extra spending money needed: _____

_____

_____

Weather temperatures: _____

_____

Clothing I will need to take: _____

_____

_____

14-3

©1987 by The Center for Applied Research in Education, Inc.

NAME _____   **DATE** _____

THINGS I SHOULD KNOW FOR THE TRIP
(continued)

Different foods I might eat: _____

_____

_____

Kinds of items I can shop for: _____

_____

_____

Other things to know before leaving on this trip:

_____

_____

_____

_____

_____

_____

NAME _____   **DATE** _____

ITINERARY: DAY ONE

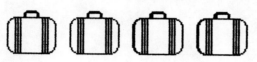

Date: _____

Time we leave: _____

Where we eat: Breakfast _____

Lunch _____

Dinner _____

Map showing the route we take today:

Points of interest (draw pictures or write about them):

Other things to see and do today: _____

_____

_____

Where we stay tonight: _____

Special instructions for tomorrow: _____

_____

NAME _____   **DATE** _____

ITINERARY: DAY TWO

Date: _____

Time we leave: _____

Where we eat: Breakfast _____

Lunch _____

Dinner _____

Map showing the route we take today:

Points of interest (draw pictures or write about them):

Other things to see and do today: _____

_____

_____

Where we stay tonight: _____

Special instructions for tomorrow: _____

_____

NAME _____   DATE _____

ITINERARY: DAY THREE

Date: _____

Time we leave: _____

Where we eat: Breakfast _____

Lunch _____

Dinner _____

Map showing the route we take today:

Points of interest (draw pictures or write about them):

Other things to see and do today: _____

_____

_____

Where we stay tonight: _____

Special instructions for tomorrow: _____

_____

NAME _____ **DATE** _____

ITINERARY: DAY FOUR

Date: _____

Time we leave: _____

Where we eat: Breakfast _____

Lunch _____

Dinner _____

Map showing the route we take today:

Points of interest (draw pictures or write about them):

Other things to see and do today: _____

_____

_____

Where we stay tonight: _____

Special instructions for tomorrow: _____

_____

NAME _____ **DATE** _____

ITINERARY: DAY FIVE

Date: _____

Time we leave: _____

Where we eat: Breakfast _____

Lunch _____

Dinner _____

Map showing the route we take today:

Points of interest (draw pictures or write about them):

Other things to see and do today: _____

_____

_____

Where we stay tonight: _____

Special instructions for tomorrow: _____

_____

REMEMBER, THIS IS THE LAST TOUR DAY.

NAME _____   GRADE _____

Research Report #15

FAMOUS PEOPLE AROUND THE WORLD

TEACHER _____   DATE _____

NAME _____   DATE _____

Project Instructions

This research report is to be done on a famous person. This person may be living or dead and may have been born anywhere in the world.

1. You may choose a book to read about a famous person or use encyclopedias and other reference sources. Your teacher or librarian may wish to help you.

2. Read the questions on the next pages very carefully. Then read your book or other sources, keeping those questions in mind.

3. After you have finished your reading, answer each question in your own words, using good sentences.

4. Complete the part of the bibliography page that applies to you.

5. Design your own title page or use the one provided with this research report.

NAME _____   DATE _____

THE PERSON I'M WRITING ABOUT

I chose to read about _____

Draw or find a picture of your famous person to paste on the chalkboard below.

ABCDEFGHIJKLMNOPQRSTUVWXYZ

Your teacher or librarian will assist you if you need help.

NAME _____   **DATE** _____

ABOUT THE PERSON

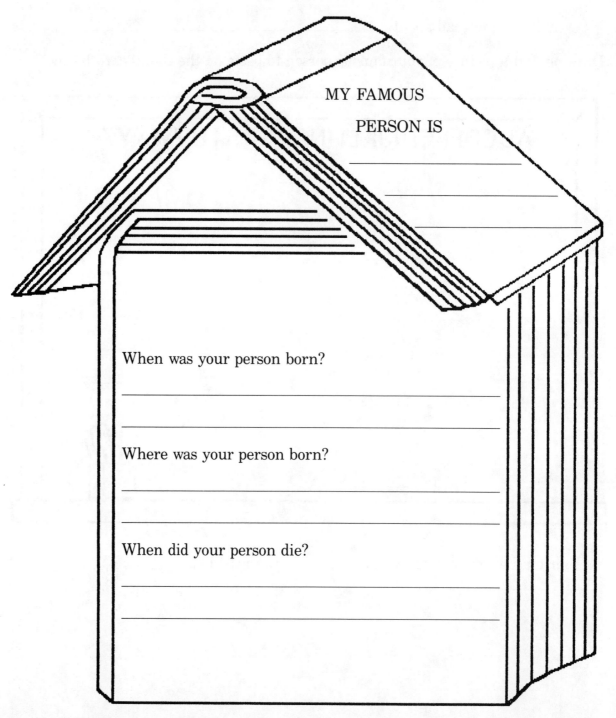

MY FAMOUS

PERSON IS

_____

_____

_____

When was your person born?

_____

_____

Where was your person born?

_____

_____

When did your person die?

_____

_____

DON'T FORGET TO WRITE YOUR FACTS IN GOOD SENTENCES!

NAME _____   DATE _____

AT HOME OR ABROAD?

Where did your person live during his or her lifetime?

_____
_____
_____
_____
_____
_____
_____
_____
_____

Tell about the country, cities, or small towns your person lived in while growing up.

NAME _____   DATE _____

FAMILY LIFE

Tell all about your famous person's family:

Name each member of the family. How many brothers and sisters were there? Were they older or younger than your famous person? Tell about different things they did together while growing up.

NAME _____   DATE _____

THE PERSON'S ACCOMPLISHMENTS

What was your person famous for?

_____
_____
_____
_____
_____
_____
_____
_____
_____
_____
_____
_____
_____
_____

NAME _____   DATE _____

OTHER INTERESTING FACTS

Use this sheet to write down other interesting facts you learned about your famous person.

NAME _____   DATE _____

BIBLIOGRAPHY PAGE

Fill in the following information if you read a book for this research report.

BIBLIOGRAPHY
Title of Book : _____
_____
Author : _____
Publisher: _____
Copyright Date: _____
Number of Pages: _____

Fill in the following information if you used an encyclopedia or other source.

BIBLIOGRAPHY

Source No. 1: _____

Title: _____

Author: _____

Page Number (s) _____

Copyright: _____ Vol. No. (s)_____

Source No 2 : _____

Title: _____

Author: _____

Page Number (s) _____

Copyright: _____ Vol. No. (s)_____

Activity Pages

to

Accompany Section III

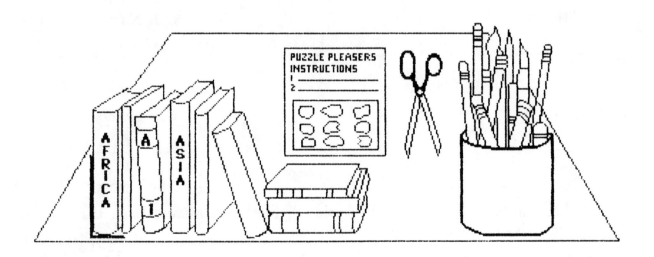

©1987 by The Center for Applied Research in Education, Inc.

NAME _____   DATE _____

BOOKS ABOUT PEOPLE

Books about famous people are called biographies. They are true stories based on facts about a person. There are two kinds of biography books in the library:

1. Individual biographies are books containing information about the life of one person.
2. Collective biographies are books containing information about the lives of several persons.

Some libraries use the letter B for biography books. Other libraries use 921 for individual biographies and 920 for collective biographies. Check your library and see how your biography section is arranged. Ask your librarian to explain it for you if you don't understand it.

Now, find two individual biography books on the shelves in your library. Write down the title of each book and the call number.

1. Title   Call Number

_____   _____

_____

2. Title   Call Number

_____   _____

_____

Find one book in the biography section that looks interesting. Read it! Then write five facts about your famous person below.

My famous person is _____

Five facts are:

1. _____

2. _____

3. _____

4. _____

5. _____

Read your facts to friends or classmates, but don't give them the name of your person. See if they can guess the famous person you read about.

NAME _____   **DATE** _____

CLOTHING PEOPLE WEAR

Identify these people by the clothing they wear:

Dutch	Italian	Chinese	Scottish	Japanese	Hawaiian

_____   _____   _____

Color the clothing these people are wearing.

TRUE or FALSE. Circle the correct answer:

1. Clothing is worn to protect the body.   T   F
2. Heavy clothing is needed in warm climates.   T   F
3. Some people wear clothes made of skins.   T   F
4. All people wear the same kind of clothing.   T   F
5. Clothing can be made from many different materials.   T   F

On the back of this sheet, list three ways in which climate affects the clothing we wear.

A MAP OF THE LIBRARY

Can you find your way around your school library? Cut along the dotted line. Cut out the items below and place them where they would go on the map. Add other items too, so it will look more like your library. Show your favorite reading spot.

CARD CATALOG

TABLE   TABLE   TABLE   BOOKS

DESK   TABLE   TABLE   TABLE   BOOKS

BOOKS   BOOKS   MAGAZINES

NAME _____   DATE _____

LIBRARY FLOOR PLAN

Visit your school library. Study it very carefully. Then draw up a floor plan. Include these items in your plan:

—Card Catalog
—Fiction Book Section
—Librarian's Desk
—Magazine Section
—Nonfiction Book Section

—Reading Tables
—Reference Books
—Anything else
 that you find in
 your library

NAME _____   DATE _____

A MAP OF AGRICULTURAL PRODUCTS

Choose a country, state, or province. Draw or trace a map of it. Show the most important agricultural products grown there. Be sure your map has a title and legend. Your teacher or librarian may offer other suggestions as well.

AGRICULTURAL PRODUCTS: foods produced from farming.

NAME _____   DATE _____

A MAP OF NATURAL RESOURCES

GAS
OIL

GEMS

MINERALS

    Choose a country, state, or province. Draw or trace a map of it. Show the most important natural resources found there. Be sure your map has a title and legend. Your teacher or librarian may offer other suggestions as well.

NATURAL RESOURCES: forms of wealth supplied by nature, such as coal, oil, and ore.

A MAP OF RAINFALL

Choose a country, state, or province. Draw or trace a map of it. Show the rainfall for that area. Be sure your map has a title and legend. Your teacher or librarian may offer other suggestions as well.

RAINFALL: amount of rain that falls in different areas during the seasons.

NAME _____   DATE _____

A MAP OF YOUR STREET

Draw a map of part of the street where you live. Show your house and the neighbor's house on each side of you. You might like to show some houses on the other side of the street too. Be sure your map has a title, directions, and a legend. Your teacher or librarian may offer other suggestions as well.

LEGEND

.... House

.... School

.... Church

...... Railroad

.... Road

.... Tree

.... Park

LEGEND: explanation or description of the meaning of the symbols used on a map.

NAME _____   DATE _____

GEOGRAPHY FACTS

Go to the library. Find the *World Almanac and Book of Facts* (1986) to help you answer the following questions in geography. Get your teacher or librarian to help you, if you need assistance.

Find page 432 in your almanac. Answer the following:

1. What is the longest river in the U.S.? _____

   How long is it? _____

2. Name the highest mountain. _____

   How high is it? _____

3. What is the smallest state? _____

4. Name the oldest national park. _____

5. Where is the deepest lake found? _____

Now, turn to page 705 in the almanac. Answer the following:

1. Name the capital of Nova Scotia. _____

2. What is the population of Thunder Bay, Ontario? _____

3. Where is the highest town in Canada found? _____

4. What is the capital of Ontario? _____

5. Name the longest river. _____

   How long is it? _____

Browse through the rest of the almanac. Write down two interesting geography facts that you found on other pages.

1. _____

2. _____

If you don't have an almanac to use, get your teacher or librarian to suggest other reference sources.

NAME _____   DATE _____

GEOGRAPHY TERMS

In order to do a neat job, use a ruler!

Match these geography terms by drawing a line from the term to the correct definition.

1. Bay   a body of water, larger than a bay, partly enclosed by land

2. Canyon   a body of land completely surrounded by water

3. Island   a body of water partly closed off to the sea by land

4. Continent   when land and water meet on a shoreline

5. Cape   a large body of water surrounded by land

6. Coastline   a valley with steep sides or cliffs

7. Ocean   a point of land that projects into a sea, lake, or coastline

8. Gulf   one of seven land masses on the earth's surface

9. River   a body of salt water that covers 72 percent of the earth's surface

10. Lake   a large stream that empties into a lake, ocean, or body of water

Write down a place name for each.

1. a cape _____   6. a continent _____

2. a bay _____   7. an ocean _____

3. a canyon _____   8. a river _____

4. an island _____   9. a coastline _____

5. a lake _____   10. a gulf _____

You might like to check your answers by using a geography dictionary or other reference sources suggested by your teacher or librarian.

That was as easy as water running off a duck's back!

NAME _____   **DATE** _____

HOLIDAYS AROUND THE WORLD

Choose a country from around the world.

I chose _____

List five holidays that are important to the people of that country and the dates that they are held on.

1. _____

2. _____

3. _____

4. _____

5. _____

Tell why one of these holidays is important or what historical or religious significance it has:

_____

_____

_____

_____

_____

_____

_____

_____

_____

_____

_____

_____

_____

NAME _____   DATE _____

CANADIAN ABBREVIATIONS

Use your ATLAS to help you with the spelling.

This map of Canada shows the ten provinces and two territories that make up the country. Abbreviations have been used on the map. Write the complete word for the province or territory below.

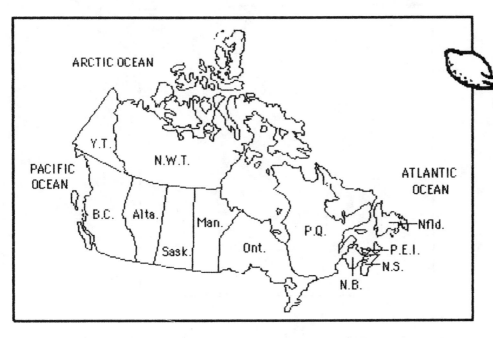

ARCTIC OCEAN

PACIFIC OCEAN

Y.T.

N.W.T.

B.C.   Alta.

Man.

Sask.

Ont.

P.Q.

ATLANTIC OCEAN

Nfld.

P.E.I.

N.S.

N.B.

1. Alta. _____

2. B.C. _____

3. Man. _____

4. N.B. _____

5. Nfld. _____

6. P.Q. _____

7. N.S. _____

8. Ont. _____

9. P.E.I. _____

10. Sask. _____

11. N.W.T. _____

12. Y.T. _____

Now, can you name the five Great Lakes?

1. Lake _____

2. Lake _____

3. Lake _____

4. Lake _____

5. Lake _____

I hope you answered the question on the GREAT LAKES, too. That means you've tried to do a SUPER JOB!

NAME _____   DATE _____

EASTERN U.S. ABBREVIATIONS

This map of the United States shows 26 states with the abbreviations used for each state name. Locate each state on the map. Then write the full state name below.

BE BRAVE!
Try to do
this page
by yourself,
if you can.

1. WI _____

2. IL _____

3. MS _____

4. MI _____

5. IN _____

6. TN _____

7. AL _____

8. KY _____

9. OH _____

10. WV _____

11. GA _____

12. FL _____

13. SC _____

14. NC _____

15. VA _____

16. MD _____

17. PA _____

18. NY _____

19. DE _____

20. NJ _____

21. CT _____

22. RI _____

23. MA _____

24. NH _____

25. VT _____

26. ME _____

Use your
ATLAS to
assist you,
if you are
in trouble.

Did that make
you feel better?

NAME _____   DATE _____

WESTERN U.S. ABBREVIATIONS

This map of the United States shows 24 states with the abbreviations used for each state name. Locate each state on the map. Then write the full state name below.

You should know where to find these states, after doing this. GOOD LUCK!

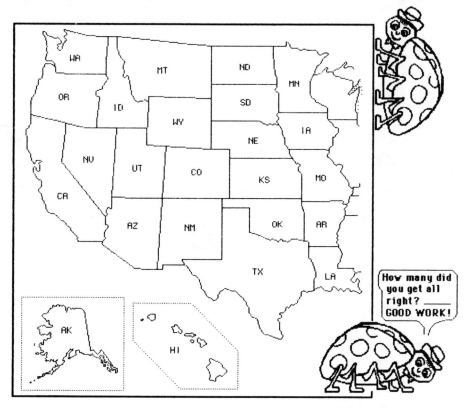

How many did you get all right? _____ GOOD WORK!

1. WA _____
2. OR _____
3. CA _____
4. NV _____
5. ID _____
6. UT _____
7. AZ _____
8. MT _____

9. WY _____
10. CO _____
11. NM _____
12. ND _____
13. SD _____
14. NE _____
15. KS _____
16. OK _____

17. TX _____
18. AK _____
19. HI _____
20. MN _____
21. IA _____
22. MO _____
23. AR _____
24. LA _____

Do as much of this page as you can by yourself. Use an atlas if you need help.

NAME _____   DATE _____

NATIONAL LANDMARKS

Choose a country. Find information on the landmarks of that country. Write a story and draw a picture of two of them.

1. _____

2. _____

NAME _____   **DATE** _____

PLAN A MENU

Pretend you own a restaurant. Make up a menu below that gives a selection of foods which are specialties of a certain country. List three entrees, five main courses, three desserts, and two beverages. Design your menu so that it represents the culture and life of that country.

NAME _____   DATE _____

AFRICA PUZZLE PLEASERS

INSTRUCTIONS:

1. Cut out your puzzle pieces very carefully.

2. Rearrange the puzzle pieces so that the puzzle fits together to form the continent of Africa.

3. You may then glue them on heavier paper if you wish.

4. Check with your teacher to see if it is done correctly or look in your atlas.

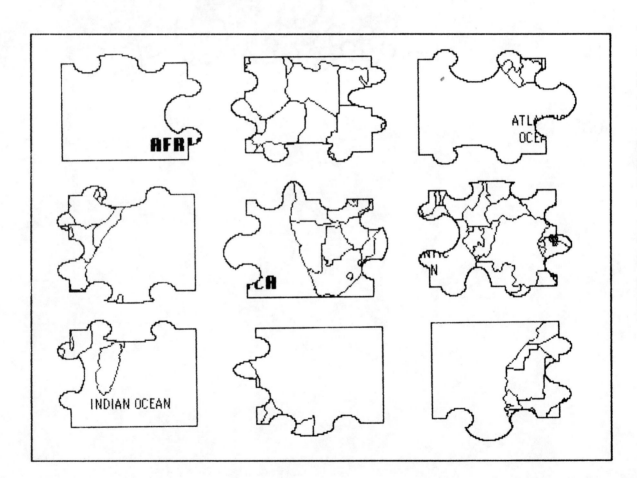

NAME _____   DATE _____

ASIA PUZZLE PLEASERS

INSTRUCTIONS:

1. Cut out your puzzle pieces very carefully.

2. Rearrange the puzzle pieces so that the puzzle fits together to form the continent of Asia.

3. You may then glue them on heavier paper if you wish.

4. Check with your teacher to see if it is done correctly or look in your atlas.

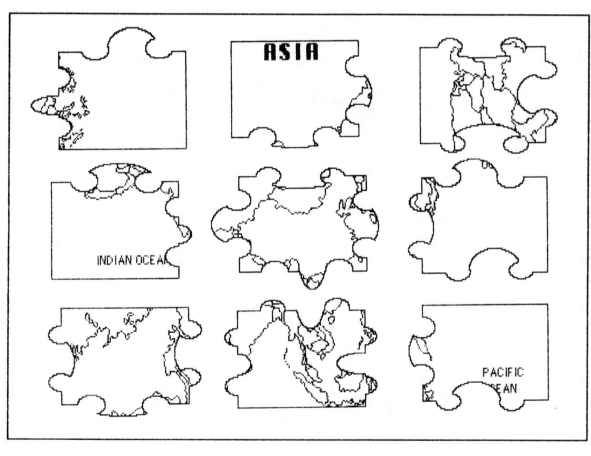

NAME _____   DATE _____

AUSTRALIA PUZZLE PLEASERS

INSTRUCTIONS:

1. Cut out your puzzle pieces very carefully.

2. Rearrange the puzzle pieces so that the puzzle fits together to form the continent of Australia.

3. You may then glue them on heavier paper if you wish.

4. Check with your teacher to see if it is done correctly or look in your atlas.

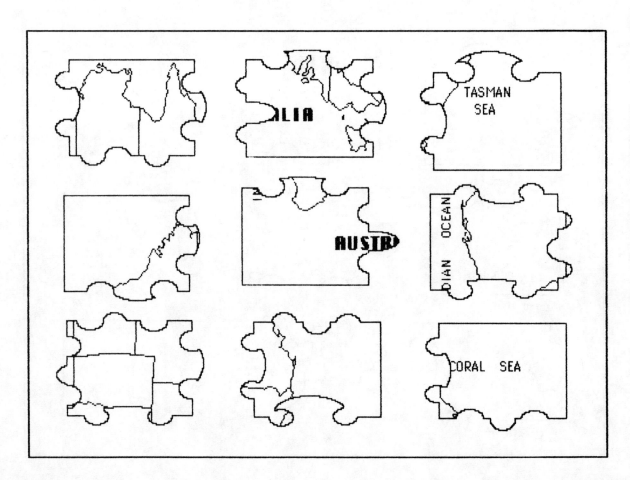

NAME _____   DATE _____

EUROPE PUZZLE PLEASERS

INSTRUCTIONS:

1. Cut out your puzzle pieces very carefully.

2. Rearrange the puzzle pieces so that the puzzle fits together to form the continent of Europe.

3. You may then glue them on heavier paper if you wish.

4. Check with your teacher to see if it is done correctly or look in your atlas.

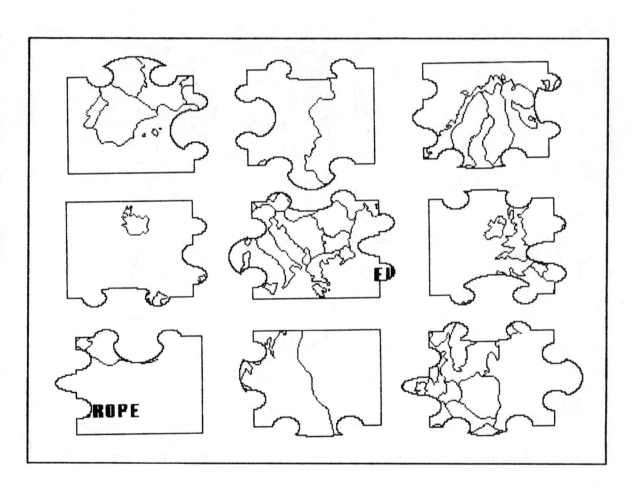

NORTH AMERICA PUZZLE PLEASERS

INSTRUCTIONS:

1. Cut out your puzzle pieces very carefully.

2. Rearrange the puzzle pieces so that the puzzle fits together to form the continent of North America.

3. You may then glue them on heavier paper if you wish.

4. Check with your teacher to see if it is done correctly or look in your atlas.

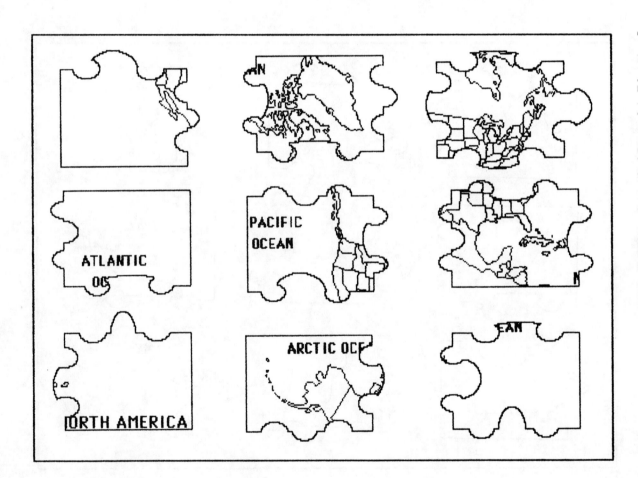

NAME _____   DATE _____

SOUTH AMERICA PUZZLE PLEASERS

INSTRUCTIONS:

1. Cut out your puzzle pieces very carefully.

2. Rearrange the puzzle pieces so that the puzzle fits together to form the continent of South America.

3. You may then glue them on heavier paper if you wish.

4. Check with your teacher to see if it is done correctly or look in your atlas.

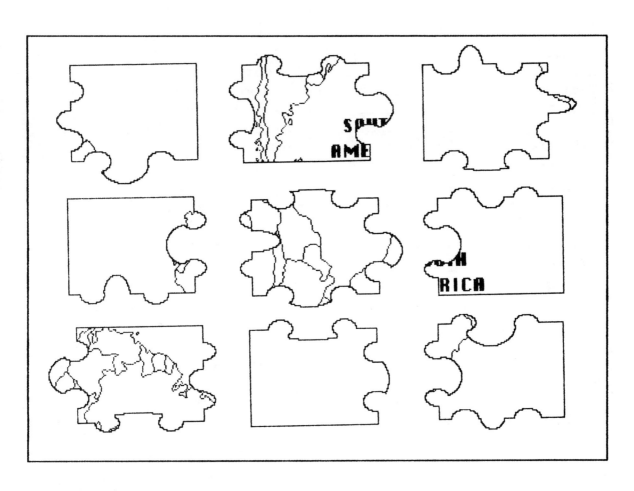

NAME _____   **DATE** _____

QUICK QUIZ ON AFRICA

Africa — EGYPT
ETHIOPIA
ZAIRE
SOUTH AFRICA

Go to your library. Find the reference section. Use the reference book, *Lands and People,* as your source for answering the questions below.

FACTS AND FIGURES
Look up EGYPT
Capital: _____
Language: _____
Religion: _____
Chief cities: _____
_____
2 imports: _____
2 exports: _____
National holiday: _____
_____
Monetary unit: _____
_____

FACTS AND FIGURES
Look up ETHIOPIA
Capital: _____
Language: _____
Religion: _____
Chief cities: _____
_____
2 imports: _____
2 exports: _____
National holiday: _____
_____
Monetary unit: _____
_____

FACTS AND FIGURES
Look up SOUTH AFRICA
Capital: _____
Language: _____
Religion: _____
Chief cities: _____
_____
2 imports: _____
2 exports: _____
National holiday: _____
_____
Monetary unit: _____
_____

FACTS AND FIGURES
Look up ZAIRE
Capital: _____
Language: _____
Religion: _____
Chief cities: _____
_____
2 imports: _____
2 exports: _____
National holiday: _____
_____
Monetary unit: _____
_____

GR-R-R-EAT JOB!

Answer the following questions on the back of this sheet.

1. What is the population of Africa?
2. Name the highest and lowest points of land.
3. List three chief rivers of Africa.

You may find these answers in your encyclopedias, too.

NAME _____ DATE _____

QUICK QUIZ ON ASIA

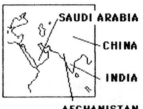

Go to your library. Find the reference section. Use the reference book, *Lands and People,* as your source for answering the questions below.

FACTS AND FIGURES
Look up AFGHANISTAN

Capital: _____

Language: _____

2 Religions: _____

_____

Chief cities: _____

_____

2 imports: _____

2 exports: _____

_____

Monetary unit: _____

_____

FACTS AND FIGURES
Look up CHINA

Capital: _____

Language: _____

2 Religions: _____

_____

Chief cities: _____

_____

2 imports: _____

2 exports: _____

_____

Monetary unit: _____

_____

FACTS AND FIGURES
Look up INDIA

Capital: _____

Language: _____

2 Religions: _____

_____

Chief cities: _____

_____

2 imports: _____

2 exports: _____

_____

Monetary unit: _____

_____

FACTS AND FIGURES
Look up SAUDI ARABIA

Capital: _____

Language: _____

2 Religions: _____

_____

Chief cities: _____

_____

2 imports: _____

2 exports: _____

_____

Monetary unit: _____

_____

Answer the following questions on the back of this sheet.

1. What is the population of Asia?
2. Name the highest and lowest points of land.
3. List three chief rivers of Asia.
4. Name four other countries found in Asia.

You may find these answers in your encyclopedias, too.

NAME _____   DATE _____

QUICK QUIZ ON AUSTRALIA

I live only in Australia. What is my name?

Go to your library. Find the reference section. Use the reference book, *Lands and People,* as your source for answering the questions below.

FACTS AND FIGURES

Look up AUSTRALIA
What is the official name of the country?

_____

Name the capital: _____

Language spoken: _____

List the chief cities: _____

_____

Monetary unit used: _____

National holiday: _____

National anthem: _____

_____

Religion: _____

Population: _____

3 chief minerals: _____

3 chief imports: _____

3 chief exports: _____

Mark Australia's states and territories on this map:

New South Wales, Victoria, Queensland, South Australia, Western Australia, Northern Territory, and Tasmania.

NAME _____   **DATE** _____

QUICK QUIZ ON EUROPE

   Go to your library. Find the reference section. Use the reference book, *Lands and People,* as your source for answering the questions below.

FACTS AND FIGURES

Look up ENGLAND

Capital: _____

Language: _____

Religion: _____

Chief cities: _____

_____

2 imports: _____

2 exports: _____

National holiday: _____

_____

Monetary unit: _____

_____

FACTS AND FIGURES

Look up FRANCE

Capital: _____

Language: _____

Religion: _____

Chief cities: _____

_____

2 imports: _____

2 exports: _____

National holiday: _____

_____

Monetary unit: _____

_____

FACTS AND FIGURES

Look up ITALY

Capital: _____

Language: _____

Religion: _____

Chief cities: _____

_____

2 imports: _____

2 exports: _____

National holiday: _____

_____

Monetary unit: _____

_____

FACTS AND FIGURES

Look up SWITZERLAND

Capital: _____

Language: _____

Religion: _____

Chief cities: _____

_____

2 imports: _____

2 exports: _____

National holiday: _____

_____

Monetary unit: _____

_____

Answer the following questions on the back of this sheet.

1. Which country is not part of mainland Europe?
2. List four rivers found in mainland Europe.
3. What is the lowest point on the mainland?
4. Name three countries where you can climb mountains in Europe.

You may find these answers in your encyclopedias, too.

NAME _____   DATE _____

QUICK QUIZ ON NORTH AMERICA

Go to your library. Find the reference section. Use the reference book, *Lands and People,* as your source for answering the questions below.

FACTS AND FIGURES
Look up BAHAMAS
Capital: _____
Language: _____
Religion: _____
Chief cities: _____

2 imports: _____
2 exports: _____
National holiday: _____

Monetary unit: _____

FACTS AND FIGURES
Look up CANADA
Capital: _____
Language: _____
Religion: _____
Chief cities: _____

2 imports: _____
2 exports: _____
National holiday: _____

Monetary unit: _____

FACTS AND FIGURES
Look up MEXICO
Capital: _____
Language: _____
Religion: _____
Chief cities: _____

2 imports: _____
2 exports: _____
National holiday: _____

Monetary unit: _____

FACTS AND FIGURES
Look up UNITED STATES
Capital: _____
Language: _____
Religion: _____
Chief cities: _____

2 imports: _____
2 exports: _____
National holiday: _____

Monetary unit: _____

Answer the following questions on the back of this sheet.

1. What is the population of North America?
2. Name the highest and lowest points of land.
3. List four chief rivers of North America.
4. Name the national symbol of the United States and of Canada.

You may find these answers in your encyclopedias, too.

NAME _____   DATE _____

QUICK QUIZ ON SOUTH AMERICA

Go to your library. Find the reference section. Use the reference book, *Lands and People,* as your source for answering the questions below.

FACTS AND FIGURES
Look up ARGENTINA
Capital: _____
Language: _____
Religion: _____
Chief cities: _____

_____
2 imports: _____
2 exports: _____
National holiday: _____

_____
Monetary unit: _____

_____

FACTS AND FIGURES
Look up BRAZIL
Capital: _____
Language: _____
Religion: _____
Chief cities: _____

_____
2 imports: _____
2 exports: _____
National holiday: _____

_____
Monetary unit: _____

FACTS AND FIGURES
Look up PERU
Capital: _____
Language: _____
Religion: _____
Chief cities: _____

_____
2 imports: _____
2 exports: _____
National holiday: _____

_____
Monetary unit: _____

_____

FACTS AND FIGURES
Look up VENEZUELA
Capital: _____
Language: _____
Religion: _____
Chief cities: _____

_____
2 imports: _____
2 exports: _____
National holiday: _____

_____
Monetary unit: _____

Answer the following questions on the back of this sheet.

I am a Y_____
My cousin is a llama. Do you know who I am?

1. What is the population of South America?
2. Name the highest and lowest points of land.
3. List three chief rivers of South America.

You may find these answers in your encyclopedias, too.

NAME _____   DATE _____

SURVEY OF A CITY

Choose a city from around the world. List five interesting things to see or do in that city.

I chose _____

Five interesting things to see or do are:

1. _____

2. _____

3. _____

4. _____

5. _____

Draw pictures of the interesting things you did. Label your drawings.

NAME _____   DATE _____

SURVEY OF A COUNTRY

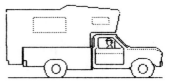

Choose a country from around the world. List five interesting things to see or do in that country.

I chose _____

Five interesting things to see or do are:

1. _____

2. _____

3. _____

4. _____

5. _____

Draw pictures of the interesting things you did. Label your drawings.

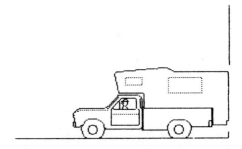

NAME _____   DATE _____

SURVEY OF A PROVINCE

Choose a province from the country of Canada. List five interesting things to see or do in that province.

I chose _____

Five interesting things to see or do are:

1. _____

2. _____

3. _____

4. _____

5. _____

Draw pictures of the interesting things you did. Label your drawings.

NAME _____   DATE _____

SURVEY OF A STATE

Choose one state in the United States. List five interesting things to see or do in that state.

I chose _____

Five interesting things to see or do are:

1. _____

2. _____

3. _____

4. _____

5. _____

Draw pictures of the interesting things you did. Label your drawings.

NAME _____   **DATE** _____

USING THE ATLAS

The atlas is a very important reference book that contains a collection of maps.

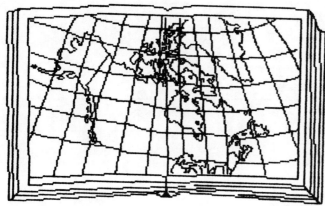

Check your classroom or school library. Find two atlases that you might use. Fill in the information below:

1. Title: _____

   Publisher: _____

   Year of Publication: _____

2. Title: _____

   Publisher: _____

   Year of Publication: _____

   Now, use one of the atlases to find a map that shows the country, state, or province where you live. Fill in the information below:

Place where you live: _____

Name of atlas: _____

Page number of map: _____

   Your teacher or librarian will assist you, if you need help.

NAME _____   **DATE** _____

MAPS IN AN ATLAS

We sure could have used an ATLAS!

Some maps in an atlas show the physical geography of a country such as the mountains, lakes, rivers, and deserts.

Political maps show state and provincial boundaries, capital cities, and other important places.

Some atlases have special maps that show the products, population, rainfall, and temperature of a country.

Now, use an atlas to find a map that shows the country where you live. Fill in the information below:

Name of country: _____

State or province: _____

Name of atlas: _____

Page number of map: _____

Find a physical map showing mountains, lakes, etc. Fill in the information below:

Name of map: _____

Name of atlas: _____

Page number of map: _____

Find a political map of North America showing the boundaries between countries. Fill in the information:

Name of map: _____

Name of atlas: _____

Page number of map: _____

POLLY says PERFECT!

NAME _____   DATE _____

AN ITINERARY CHECKLIST

Pretend that you and a friend are going on a trip to
Europe. With a red marker, trace the numbered route from
one to fourteen that you will follow. Use an atlas to help you
find the missing names.

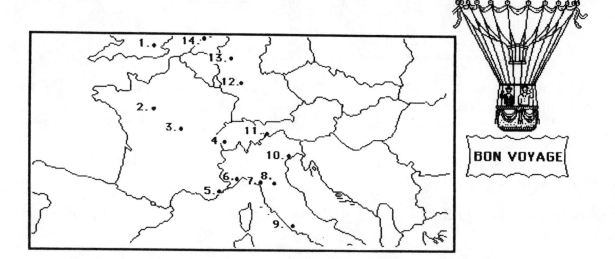

BON VOYAGE

_____ and I flew from San Francisco, over the Atlantic Ocean, to
(1) _____ , England (capital). After several days of sightseeing we boarded a
plane which flew us to (2) _____ , France (capital). There we saw the Eiffel
Tower and took a boat ride on the River Seine. We left this beautiful city and headed
southeast to (3) Dijon, then on to (4) Geneva, which is in the country of
_____ . The next day we drove south to the sunny Mediterranean and
spent a day on the beach at (5) _____ , on the French Riviera. The next
morning, we crossed the border into Italy, traveled through (6) Genoa, then south to
(7) _____ , where we got a chance to see the leaning tower. After a short bus
ride we arrived in (8) Florence. From there, we traveled south to (9) _____ ,
Italy (capital.) After several exciting days, we went back to Florence, then on to
(10) _____ , for a gondola ride. Continuing north over the Dolomites we
crossed the Brenner Pass to (11) Innsbruck, which is in _____ . This
scenic drive also included (12) Heidelberg, where we visited an old castle. We continued north to (13) Cologne, still in the country of _____ . Driving to
(14) _____ , the capital of the Netherlands, we boarded our plane, for
home, after a super trip.

NAME _____   **DATE** _____

THE INDEX IN AN ATLAS

To help you locate the maps you want, an atlas has an index which is found in the back of the book. The index is in alphabetical order and tells you the page on which each place can be found and its exact location on the map.

Find the index in your atlas. Locate the entry for each city listed below. Give the page number that you would find it on.

Name of City	Page Number
1. Aberdeen, Scotland	_____
2. Charleston, Missouri	_____
3. Digby, Nova Scotia	_____
4. Toronto, Canada	_____
5. Caracas, Venezuela	_____
6. Washington, D.C.	_____
7. London, England	_____
8. Sydney, Australia	_____
9. Athens, Greece	_____
10. Nairobi, Kenya	_____

List two other cities you found in the index. Name them and give the page number:

1. _____   _____

2. _____   _____

NAME _____   DATE _____

WHERE WOULD YOU BE? A AND B

You need to know your alphabet when using an INDEX.

Column A gives the names of places starting with the letters A or B, found anywhere in the world. Column B gives the name of the country, province, or state that place may be found in.

Practice using the index of a world atlas by checking the names of each place. Then print the correct letter and word beside each number to show where you would be in the world. The first one is done for you.

Column A

_g_   1. Abitibi, ___Ontario___   a. Alaska

_____ 2. Alpine, _____   b. India

_____ 3. Bangor, _____   c. Michigan

_____ 4. Adelaide, _____   d. Ohio

_____ 5. Birch River, _____   e. New Zealand

_____ 6. Anchorage, _____   f. Maine

_____ 7. Brookfield, _____   g. Ontario

_____ 8. Akron, _____   h. Australia

_____ 9. Ashburton, _____   i. Manitoba

_____ 10. Bay City, _____   j. Texas

_____ 11. Abu, _____   k. Missouri

_____ 12. Burlington, _____   l. New Jersey

Column B

Have some more fun by trying to locate these places on a map.

I hope you tried to find these places on your maps, too!

NAME _____   DATE _____

WHERE WOULD YOU BE? D AND E

Check your names very carefully, so you won't be fooled!

Column A gives the names of places starting with the letters D or E, found anywhere in the world. Column B gives the name of the country, province, or state that place may be found in.

Practice using the index of a world atlas by checking the names of each place. Then print the correct letter and word beside each number to show where you would be in the world. The first one is done for you.

Column A

©1987 by The Center for Applied Research in Education, Inc.

Column B

___f___   1. Dade City, ___Florida___   a. Zaire

_____   2. Elm, _____   b. Alaska

_____   3. Dixon, _____   c. Yukon Territories

_____   4. Englewood, _____   d. Switzerland

_____   5. Dawson, _____   e. Scotland

_____   6. Edmonton, _____   f. Florida

_____   7. Dallas, _____   g. England

_____   8. Edinburgh, _____   h. Uganda

_____   9. Dover, _____   i. New Jersey

_____   10. Entebbe, _____   j. Texas

_____   11. Dungu, _____   k. Alberta

_____   12. Eagle, _____   l. Kentucky

Where else can you find a place called Englewood?

_____

If you answered this question, you weren't catnapping!

Have some more fun by trying to locate these places on a map.

NAME _____   DATE _____

WHERE WOULD YOU BE? O AND P

Column A gives the names of places starting with the letters O or P, found anywhere in the world. Column B gives the name of the country, province, or state that place may be found in.

Practice using the index of a world atlas by checking the names of each place. Then print the correct letter and word beside each number to show where you would be in the world. The first one is done for you.

Column A   Column B

___g___ 1. Oakland, ___California___   a. Utah

_____ 2. Palmas, _____   b. Kansas

_____ 3. Paris, _____   c. Michigan

_____ 4. Ocala, _____   d. Brazil

_____ 5. Paradise Valley, _____   e. Ontario

_____ 6. Ogden, _____   f. France

_____ 7. Onaway, _____   g. California

_____ 8. Prestwick, _____   h. Alberta

_____ 9. Owen Sound, _____   i. Florida

_____ 10. Pisa, _____   j. New Jersey

_____ 11. Oakley, _____   k. Italy

_____ 12. Plainfield, _____   l. Scotland

Have some more fun by trying to locate these places on a map.

NAME _____   DATE _____

WHERE WOULD YOU BE? S AND T

Column A gives the names of places starting with the letters S or T, found anywhere in the world. Column B gives the name of the country, province, or state that place may be found in.

Practice using the index of a world atlas by checking the names of each place. Then print the correct letter and word beside each number to show where you would be in the world. The first one is done for you.

Column A   Column B

___d___   1. Sable, ___France___   a. New York

_____   2. Tahta, _____   b. Saskatchewan

_____   3. Sunnyside, _____   c. Borneo

_____   4. Tarakan, _____   d. France

_____   5. St. Andrews, _____   e. Egypt

_____   6. Two Rivers, _____   f. California

_____   7. Syracuse, _____   g. Sudan

_____   8. Sacramento, _____   h. Wisconsin

_____   9. Tonga, _____   i. Scotland

_____ 10. Tokyo, _____   j. Turkey

_____ 11. Spy Hill, _____   k. Newfoundland

_____ 12. Tire, _____   l. Japan

Have some more fun by trying to locate these places on a map.

NAME _____   DATE _____

WHERE WOULD YOU BE? U AND V

Try to find all these places on the map. Be a world traveler, not a stick in the mud, like ME!

Column A gives the names of places starting with the letters U or V, found anywhere in the world. Column B gives the name of the country, province, or state that place may be found in.

Practice using the index of a world atlas by checking the names of each place. Then print the correct letter and word beside each number to show where you would be in the world. The first one is done for you.

Column A   Column B

___i___   1. Ukiah, ___California___   a. Liechtenstein

_____   2. Valletta, _____   b. India

_____   3. Venice, _____   c. Mississippi

_____   4. Utica, _____   d. Austria

_____   5. Varna, _____   e. Malta

_____   6. Una, _____   f. Georgia

_____   7. Verdun, _____   g. Indiana

_____   8. Vincennes, _____   h. Bulgaria

_____   9. Vaduz, _____   i. California

_____   10. Vienna, _____   j. New York

_____   11. Valdosta, _____   k. France

_____   12. Vicksburg, _____   l. Italy

If you know where all these places are, ask your teacher about the TERRIFIC TRAVELER AWARD!

Have some more fun by trying to locate these places on a map.

APPENDIX

Answer Keys to:

Crossword Puzzles
Word Search Puzzles
Where Would You Be?

Awards

Library ABC Award
Animal Lover Award
Research Report Award
Terrific Traveler Award
Super Student of the Week Award

MAMMALS OF AFRICA

Activity II-16

MAMMALS OF ASIA

Activity II-17

MAMMALS OF AUSTRALIA

Activity II-18

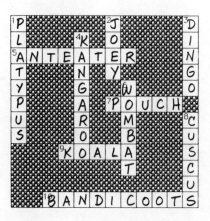

MAMMALS OF NORTH AMERICA

Activity II-19

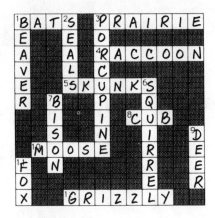

MAMMALS OF SOUTH AMERICA

Activity II-20

PETS AROUND THE WORLD

Activity II-21

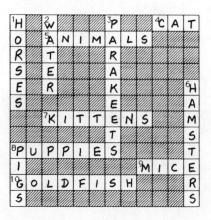

FIND THE AFRICAN MAMMALS

Activity II-34

```
T  V  A  D  O  K  A  P  I  C  N  R
N  I  R  J  R  H  R  T  S  F  O  N
A  K  H  T  H  E  E  R  E  E  I  L
H  M  F  O  I  H  R  I  P  R  L  A
P  G  E  T  N  P  D  S  O  P  K  P
E  R  N  A  O  P  O  I  L  M  O  E
L  E  N  R  C  A  M  E  L  H  N  N
E  L  E  O  E  A  H  K  T  R  E  Y
W  S  C  P  R  L  K  O  N  U  M  E
H  I  P  P  O  P  O  T  A  M  U  S
O  G  D  R  S  K  H  F  D  U  D  P
S  Z  E  B  R  A  R  T  E  P  A  I
```

FIND THE NORTH AMERICAN MAMMALS

Activity II-37

```
E  A  A  T  I  B  B  A  R  B  B  C
N  C  D  S  E  E  E  S  O  O  M  D
I  P  E  E  Q  F  A  D  C  C  B  M  R
U  C  O  C  U  A  R  R  L  B  S  R  E
C  R  S  L  I  D  B  A  D  G  E  R  E
R  O  E  R  M  R  A  B  F  A  V  S  E
O  P  A  C  R  A  E  B  R  W  O  E
P  L  D  E  E  E  P  E  R  A  L  F
A  C  R  H  L  U  D  W  X  M  R  L  O
C  H  I  P  M  U  N  K  T  F  S  W
D  R  M  X  O  S  T  A  R  W  V  L
```

FIND THE ASIAN MAMMALS

Activity II-35

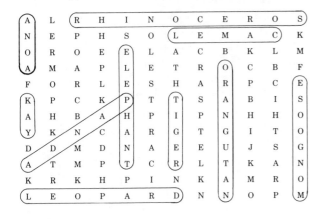

```
A  L  R  H  I  N  O  C  E  R  O  S
N  E  P  H  S  O  L  E  M  A  C  K
O  R  O  E  E  L  A  C  B  K  L  M
A  M  A  P  L  E  T  R  O  C  B  F
F  O  R  L  E  S  H  A  R  P  C  E
K  P  C  K  P  T  T  S  A  B  I  S
A  H  B  A  H  P  I  P  N  H  H  O
Y  K  N  C  R  I  G  T  G  I  T  O
D  D  M  D  N  A  E  E  U  J  S  G
A  T  M  P  T  C  R  L  T  K  A  N
K  R  K  H  P  I  N  K  A  M  R  O
L  E  O  P  A  R  D  N  A  N  O  P  M
```

FIND THE SOUTH AMERICAN MAMMALS

Activity II-38

```
J  P  S  L  O  T  H  A  S  R  L  T
B  A  G  S  O  M  L  R  H  I  P  L
C  L  G  K  E  L  S  M  R  P  S  L
D  H  H  U  M  G  H  A  P  T  A  M
P  E  C  C  A  R  Y  D  M  T  A  A
A  R  P  C  R  R  T  I  O  L  E  A
C  H  I  N  C  H  I  L  L  A  M  E
L  P  L  N  H  G  P  L  T  E  C  D
M  A  R  N  T  B  R  O  A  B  B  E
T  E  S  O  M  R  A  M  B  M  M  X
R  S  E  M  T  S  Y  M  S  P  U  T
O  C  A  N  A  U  G  E  G  T  Y  P
```

FIND THE AUSTRALIAN MAMMALS

Activity II-36

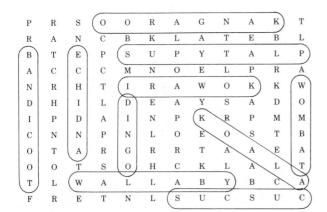

```
P  R  S  O  O  R  A  G  N  A  K  T
R  A  N  C  B  K  L  A  T  E  B  L
B  T  E  P  S  U  P  Y  T  A  L  P
A  C  C  C  M  N  O  E  L  P  R  A
N  R  H  T  I  R  A  W  O  K  K  W
D  H  I  L  D  E  A  Y  S  A  D  O
I  P  D  A  I  N  P  K  R  P  M  M
C  N  P  N  L  O  E  O  S  T  B
O  T  A  R  G  R  R  T  A  A  E  A
O  O  T  S  O  H  C  K  L  A  L  T
T  L  W  A  L  L  A  B  Y  B  C  A
F  R  E  T  N  L  S  U  C  S  U  C
```

FIND THE PETS

Activity II-39

```
P  O  R  L  T  P  S  N  E  T  A  C
U  E  L  I  Z  A  R  D  T  O  A  C
P  L  N  L  C  R  M  C  U  R  P  R
P  T  E  R  K  A  Z  P  E  L  T  A
I  R  T  M  H  K  S  U  O  N  L  B
E  U  H  N  S  E  A  Z  T  E  H  B
S  T  L  G  L  E  T  E  K  T  K  I
P  N  O  S  S  T  A  R  R  T  M  T
T  D  F  X  P  N  L  Z  M  I  N  C
R  D  A  O  T  L  R  L  O  K  S  L
I  L  H  K  X  I  Z  X  R  N  P  A
K  S  N  A  K  E  O  S  G  O  R  F
```

WHERE WOULD YOU BE? A AND B

Activity III-37

g	1.	Abitibi, Ontario
j	2.	Alpine, Texas
f	3.	Bangor, Maine
h	4.	Adelaide, Australia
i	5.	Birch River, Manitoba
a	6.	Anchorage, Alaska
k	7.	Brookfield, Missouri
d	8.	Akron, Ohio
e	9.	Ashburton, New Zealand
c	10.	Bay City, Michigan
b	11.	Abu, India
l	12.	Burlington, New Jersey

WHERE WOULD YOU BE? D AND E

Activity III-38

f	1.	Dade City, Florida
d	2.	Elm, Switzerland
l	3.	Dixon, Kentucky
i	4.	Englewood, New Jersey
c	5.	Dawson, Yukon Territories
k	6.	Edmonton, Alberta
j	7.	Dallas, Texas
e	8.	Edinburgh, Scotland
g	9.	Dover, England
h	10.	Entebbe, Uganda
a	11.	Dungu, Zaire
b	12.	Eagle, Alaska

WHERE WOULD YOU BE? O AND P

Activity III-39

g	1.	Oakland, California
d	2.	Palmas, Brazil
f	3.	Paris, France
i	4.	Ocala, Florida
h	5.	Paradise Valley, Alberta
a	6.	Ogden, Utah
c	7.	Onaway, Michigan
l	8.	Prestwick, Scotland
e	9.	Owen Sound, Ontario
k	10.	Pisa, Italy
b	11.	Oakley, Kansas
j	12.	Plainfield, New Jersey

WHERE WOULD YOU BE? S AND T

Activity III-40

d	1.	Sable, France
e	2.	Tahta, Egypt
h	3.	Sunnyside, Wisconsin
c	4.	Tarakan, Borneo
i	5.	St. Andrews, Scotland
b	6.	Two Rivers, Saskatchewan
a	7.	Syracuse, New York
f	8.	Sacramento, California
g	9.	Tonga, Sudan
l	10.	Tokyo, Japan
k	11.	Spy Hill, Newfoundland
j	12.	Tire, Turkey

WHERE WOULD YOU BE? U AND V

Activity III-41

i	1.	Ukiah, California
e	2.	Valletta, Malta
l	3.	Venice, Italy
j	4.	Utica, New York
h	5.	Varna, Bulgaria
b	6.	Una, India
k	7.	Verdun, France
g	8.	Vincennes, Indiana
a	9.	Vaduz, Liechtenstein
d	10.	Vienna, Austria
f	11.	Valdosta, Georgia
c	12.	Vicksburg, Mississippi

LIBRARY ABC AWARD

This award is
presented to

_____

for knowing the
ABC's when using
the Library.

Teacher's Name

_____

Date _____

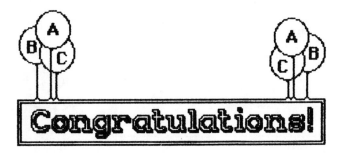

ANIMAL LOVER AWARD

WE MADE AN ANIMAL LOVER OUT OF YOU

This award is
presented

to _____

for doing such a
SUPER JOB
on the
ANIMAL REPORT
on

_____

TEACHER'S NAME: _____ **DATE:** _____

RESEARCH REPORT AWARD

HOOT-HOOT
HOORAY
FOR YOU

PRESENTED TO _____ Gr. _____

Your research report on

_____

was excellently done, and we are very proud of it.

Signed: _____ Date: _____

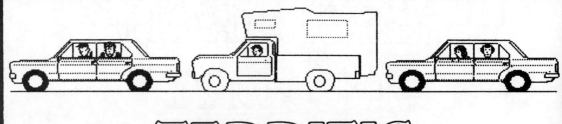

TERRIFIC TRAVELER AWARD

PRESENTED TO

_____

FOR AN EXCELLENT PROJECT ON

_____

TRAVEL AWARD

TEACHER'S NAME: _____ DATE: _____

HEAR YE! HEAR YE!

NAME

HAS BEEN CHOSEN

SUPER
STUDENT

OF THE WEEK

REASONS: _____

_____

_____

Signed: _____ Date: _____